DORSET'S WORLD HERITAGE COAST

AN ARCHAEOLOGICAL GUIDE

DORSET'S WORLD HERITAGE COAST

AN ARCHAEOLOGICAL GUIDE

JOHN BEAVIS

TEMPUS

For Brenda

First published 2004

Tempus Publishing Limited
The Mill, Brimscombe Port,
Stroud, Gloucestershire, GL5 2QG
www.tempus-publishing.com

British Library Cataloguing in Publication Data.
A catalogue record for this book is available from the British Library.

ISBN 0 7524 2545 5

Typesetting and origination by Tempus Publishing Limited
Printed in Great Britain

CONTENTS

Acknowledgements   6

Preface   7

1 Archaeology on the Dorset Coast   10

2 Chronological Outline   134

Appendix   143

Notes   148

Bibliography   152

Index   156

ACKNOWLEDGEMENTS

I am grateful to the following who took time to talk to me about aspects of the text and, in some cases supplied additional information: Alan Bailey, Peter Cox, Dr Colin Dobinson, Tony Flux, Iain Hewitt, Prof. Vincent May, Martin Papworth and Peter Woodward, and to Emma Cake who helped me with Figure 42.

PREFACE

This book was a reaction to information appearing on the World Heritage Coast that is almost all about its geology. There are guides to the natural history and history of the coast, and guides to its 'sights', and those which deal with the well-known places along the coast, and with the archaeology of the larger region. But there is nothing specifically on the archaeology of the coast and this book attempts to fill that gap. I did not want to write a 'typical' archaeological guide containing a gazetteer of formulaic accounts, which usually fail to give a fair taste of what it feels like to encounter archaeological evidence in the landscape. What is an archaeological site, anyway? Guidebooks imply they know, because they usually confine themselves to sites that are 'worthy': more or less striking, well-known, and about which something 'interesting' can be said, usually something that seems like sound knowledge.

For me, meeting archaeological evidence in the field – by which I mean the physical evidence of past human activity detectable without excavation – is much more like attempting to solve a puzzle. What I find interesting is trying to infer as much as possible from the evidence I can see, relating it to my rather unsystematic knowledge of similar kinds of evidence, trying to work out why the landscape looks the way it does, particularly in terms of human activity. It seems much more fun to try to 'read' the landscape first and, only then to turn to what other people might have said about it, or to primary data from aerial photography, geophysics and excavation, and to documentary and even personal recollection for more recent times. This may not quite be respectable scholarship, but it is serious fun. And simply because it is fun, and more engaging than being told things about the landscape, I have written this guide from the perspective of a landscape investigator, walking along the coastal path from Studland in the east to Lyme Regis in the west, puzzling over what catches the attention.

If you walk along any stretch of coast you encounter evidence from all periods in no particular order: how can a guide based on a walk deal coherently with the chronology of the evidence? It cannot directly, but in an attempt to limit confusion, I have included a brief chronological summary of the main human influences on landscape from earliest times to the present, and cross-referenced this to sites encountered on the coast. How expert is your guide? Can I claim to deal authoritatively with the huge range of evidence: domestic, ritual, military, industrial; over all periods: from prehistoric and Romano-British through Medieval and post-Medieval to the twentieth century? No, I cannot. Much of the time I will come to some approximate conclusion, usually limited by what can be seen and by my less than complete knowledge of the written sources. But I do not think this is too dangerous. After all, the quest for 'the whole truth' is a dubious ambition at the best of times, and it is arguably futile in relation to the past. This is not to say that 'anything goes' in deduction and explanation – it most definitely does not. We will take care to recognise how well arguments are supported, and when we are getting onto very thin speculative ice. Often I shall have to say: this is as far as the physical evidence can take us; and that may not be very far. Sometimes, so that the reader will not become too frustrated, I will add some inter-pretation that goes beyond what can be inferred in the field; sometimes I will emphasise a particular need for further research; sometimes we will remain just puzzled (either through personal or more widely shared ignorance). Wherever possible, I have cited references to further reading and, I have to some extent selected the excavations mentioned to illus-trate the development of this approach to investigation.

Readers must not be misled into thinking that this is the way a professional survey of the archaeology of an area would be undertaken. A systematic approach would consult all the secondary sources first; these would be followed by a study of primary documentary, photo-graphic and cartographic sources; then the field work could be carried out in an informed way. But the primary encounter in the field is often the way more careful work begins, and it is much closer to the experi-ence of people who are not professional archaeologists.

No survey of the Dorset coast, certainly not one of this scale, could pretend to cover all surviving traces of human activity that might interest any archaeologist. To limit the problem I have chosen to concentrate on the abandoned, the ruinous, the grass-covered, the bramble hidden, occasionally the completely buried: evidence which is not always easy to see or understand. Often I have left out major monuments which are still in use, have their own *in situ* interpretation, or are described in other guide books. I have also ignored conurbations, to avoid exceeding my word limit. Underwater archaeology is also omitted for the same reason. However, I have tried to include a representative selection of the evidence because I think that is more important than a carefully balanced treatment of the conventional divisions of the past, or of various categories of evidence. I am sure that readers will find some of the 'sites' discussed significant, and others quite trivial. I am also fairly sure that there will not be a high level of agreement about which sites belong to each category.

The book begins at Sandbanks Ferry, not the eastern boundary of the Dorset coast, thus appearing to ignore the whole of Poole Harbour, and eastwards to Hengistbury Head. The neglect is not as serious as it sounds. Here are three justifications for it: easily visible archaeology (as defined here) from Poole to Christchurch is swamped by urban settlement, much of the shore of Poole Harbour is inaccessible for other reasons, and the World Heritage Coast ends at Sandbanks. This is not to say it is without archaeological interest; the Romano-British pottery industry around the shores of Poole Harbour, and the Iron Age port at Hengistbury Head are significant in the wider perspective of European Archaeology, for example. Opportunities to refer to some of these topics will arise in the course of the book.

I have not assumed that readers possess more than general knowledge, but I hope they will want to discover how rich and interesting the archaeology of this stretch of coast is and, to learn the skills of reading traces of human activity in the landscape. These are skills which can be taken away and sharpened on other landscapes, not only coastal. I hope they will walk the coast path, book in hand, look at the evidence, tackle the puzzles and enjoy the experience.

Finally in the field: From time to time attention will be drawn to archaeological sites beneath your feet. *Please do not disturb these sites.* Many are scheduled ancient monuments and it is an offence to interfere with them. Occasionally, sites referred to will be on private land. *This book does not give you permission to visit them!* Often you will be examining sites near to the cliff-edge. *Take great care, and always assume that cliffs are unstable and dangerous.*

One

ARCHAEOLOGY ON THE DORSET COAST

FROM SHELL BAY TO OLD HARRY ROCKS

Follow the coast path south along the beach from the Sandbanks Ferry, turn west past the National Trust Knowle Beach café and look for an archaeological problem[1] in the south-west corner of the car park (SZ835032). (Pretend for a moment that this is a mysterious object, even if for *you* it is not; and bear with the following bit of pedantry, as it has a serious purpose!) It is a concrete structure with a flat top, six sides of unequal length, a bit bigger than a beach hut set on a slight promontory overlooking the beach *(1)*. The three adjacent sides on the north, east and south contain small rectangular depressions with their long axes horizontal, and the west side a somewhat larger rectangular depression, its long axis vertical. In the depressions the concrete is different in colour and texture from that in the rest of the structure, on the surface of which there are faint rectangular marks cast into the surface. Descriptions like this, of what can be seen, using not much more than reasonable general knowledge, is the primary skill in field archaeology. A more explanatory description, which makes more assumptions, might be: a small, flat-roofed building with thick concrete walls cast in wooden shuttering, in which there once were several small and one larger opening, now apparently blocked. Most people will have recognised this immediately and, will have unconsciously made an even greater interpretative leap, replete with assumptions, and classified the structure as a Second World War pillbox. What happened in these attempts at under-

1 A pillbox at Knowle House car park, Studland

standing? This issue is the main point of this guide, which hopes to make explicit how an archaeologist tries to observe, classify and interpret what is seen. The unconscious leap which led to 'pillbox' must have involved making some assumptions about this particular volume of space, defined in its particular concrete way, which was matched to some sort of 'pillbox' model in the mind which already 'makes sense' in your understanding of the history of twentieth-century conflict. The preceding descriptions were more cautious, drawing on more general elements of knowledge, and they would be much more appropriate if you were puzzled by the object. If you did not 'know' immediately what this thing was (and field remains will often be puzzling) what could be inferred from the evidence observed, and unspecialised knowledge? The building material in this case must be relatively recent, the hardened structure, small 'windows' (gun embrasures) facing towards the sea, an unusually small doorway facing away from it, and its position might suggest defence against something coming from the sea; a connection with a recent threat of invasion would not be an unreasonable one to make. What about the *blocked* 'windows' and door? Re-fortification against casual contemporary re-use! Such detailed exposition is probably superfluous in this case but it will be essential to adopt this stance where the diagnosis is more difficult.

2 One of the 'rings' on Studland Heath, looking north-east from the Agglestone

This pillbox is an element in the Second World War anti-invasion defences of Britain, built when a German invasion seemed likely, and particularly strong here because of the low lying beach head and entrance to Poole Harbour. There are other elements of this system to the west of the Sandbanks to Studland Road and further to the south along the beach.[2] This information provides two fragments of context for the object of interest. One is historical, the other more broadly spatial. Gathering information about the context[3] of an object is an essential part of understanding the thing itself; often, it will not be possible to gather enough contextual information to take an initial interpretation very far.

Before continuing along the path to examine some other aspects of Studland's Second World War archaeology, an excursion west from the village to the heathland landscape near the Agglestone is worthwhile, as this is the closest approach the path makes to the landscape of the Tertiary sands and gravels, the most recent geological deposits on the Heritage Coast. Some aspects of heathland archaeology which are fairly well understood will be considered later, but here there is an archaeological mystery. *Figure 2* shows an earthwork, to the north-east of the Agglestone. The figure is standing on a circular bank, which is about

10m in diameter and 30cm high, with a gap to the south-west. There are almost 100 of these in the area (and others on the heathland further west). They are likely to date between the Iron Age and the eighteenth century, but their purpose is unknown as they cannot be classified as anything domestic, defensive, industrial, agricultural or ritual known from this period (RCHM, 1970, 504); they remain a mystery. Much of the archaeological evidence encountered along the coast will not be as obscure as this but sites such as these are useful reminders that things lying beyond the boundaries of experience or record can completely frustrate attempts at interpretation. They also serve as a caution: everything from the past is more or less beyond experience, making claims for understanding always tentative, and sometimes very dubious.

Returning to the coast path near Middle Beach, there is a series of square-sided, solid concrete blocks with pyramidal tops crossing the mouth of a small valley at SZ829036 *(3)*. The arrangement creates a very serious obstacle to vehicles, and suggests that these also belong to anti-invasion defences of the Second World War. It is a line of 'Dragon's Teeth' anti-tank defences which have survived post-war demolition in this marginal location. In the background *(3, 1)* there are two concrete structures almost hidden by trees. One of these is Fort Henry. A closer

3 Anti-tank defences at Studland, with Fort Henry (1) in the background

4 Fort Henry from the south-west

inspection *(4)* shows that Fort Henry is strongly fortified and is provided with a narrow eye-level observation slit, providing a good view of Studland Bay. This reflects its role in protecting Churchill, Eisenhower and Montgomery when they observed the military exercises in prepa-ration for D-Day. These included a massive air and sea bombardment and beach assaults using live ammunition.[4]

Just to the north-west, the second concrete structure (which contains two interpretation panels) obviously differs from Fort Henry in having only three walls, the seaward side being open. This was to provide free access for traversing a coastal defence gun, the hold-fast of which is still in place on the floor. The spatial relationship between it and Fort Henry shows that the gun emplacement is earlier than the observation post, as the latter blocks the gun's field of fire. Behind the gun, steps descend to an underground magazine. One of the interesting features of this site is the original camouflage paint on the interior walls *(5)*.

South-east of Fort Henry where the coast path descends to South Beach, notice the slight terraces, elongated towards the sea, in the field to the west. These are the remains of medieval strip fields, which will be discussed more fully when some striking examples are seen near Winspit.

5 A gun emplacement beside Fort Henry

From Handfast Point, beside Old Harry Rocks, it is worth looking back at the junction between the Tertiary sands and gravels and the Cretaceous Chalk on which the path now lies, which can be well seen in the cliff section, not far from another Second World War pillbox (of different design) on the beach at Red End Point.

On turning south and starting on the gentle incline towards Ballard Point, look carefully for the slight remains of a prehistoric field system to the west of the path, which probably dates from the Iron Age and Romano-British period. The traces take the form of very low linear earthworks arranged in a roughly rectangular pattern, but the light will have to be just right (sun shining and low in the sky) for these to be seen. Another example in much better condition will be considered more fully on Kingston Down. Since the 1950s, when the Royal Commission on Historical Monuments surveyed this part of Dorset and recorded this group of fields as a well-preserved monument, ploughing has almost completely destroyed it.

View Point: Ballard Down
The concrete post on the crest of Ballard Down (SZ044813) is 'archaeological evidence' in the sense adopted here, as it has become obsolete.

It was an Ordnance Survey triangulation station, obsolete now that satellites have taken over from theodolites as the map maker's essential instrument. These can be recognised from the presence of an identifying plate near the base, usually bearing a spot height, and a bronze bearing surface on the top to locate the surveying instrument. Several others will be encountered near the path, for example: at Hambury Tout, Portland Bill, Abbotsbury Castle and Golden Cap. They are always sited in places giving excellent long distance views, and usually mark good places from which to survey the archaeological landscape, but before taking the broader view, examine some obvious earthworks nearby.

The most prominent is the bank and ditch that crosses the ridge, in archaeological language a 'cross-ridge dyke' *(colour plate 1)*. Earthworks rather like this are common in the Iron Age, often defending a promontory, just as this seems to do at first sight. What is it that makes it likely that this is much more recent, and not an attempt to defend Ballard Head? There are two obvious clues. The first is a series of iron bars projecting at the level of the old ground surface from the eastern side of the bank, which have been roughly bent over the ditch. Unless these are a careful later addition, this suggests a recent date. The second is that the ditch is to the east, on the Ballard Point side of the bank, the ineffective side, if the intention had been to fortify the headland from attack on its easy approach. A third clue, which depends on having knowledge of the form of prehistoric earthworks, is that this does not 'look right'. The ditch is very sharp edged; it has not been weathering for many generations and, on the east side, traces of shallow depressions where material seems to have been scraped up onto the bank are also rather well defined. At the north end of the earthwork is the remains of a building in 'Second World War concrete'. The lower sill of an observation window, much deeper than that at Fort Henry, is clearly visible *(6)*. This was part of the Control Post for an RAF air-to-ground firing range. [5] It appears to be later than the linear earthwork, as it is cut into it. The earthwork also contains a pit which could be a Second World War 'dug-out', also suggesting an earlier date for the earthwork. Beyond this, field deduction cannot proceed. A recent map [6] shows a disused rifle range at this point, which suggests that it may have been its butt. [7] It probably dates to the nineteenth century, or First World War.

There is a circular earthwork close to the end of the linear earthwork on the east side. This may be a temporary structure, possibly a light gun

6 An observation window of a Second World War air-to-ground firing range control post, Ballard Down

emplacement, dating to the Second World War *(colour plate 2)*, but it has also been suggested[8] that it could be connected with a Napoleonic signalling station shown on an early nineteenth-century map. Further discussion of this type of site will be deferred until other examples are encountered further west (e.g. at Round Down).

Turning to the broader view to the north from this point, the landscape of the Tertiary rocks beyond Studland and that of the Chalk of Ballard Down can be compared *(7)*. The former, largely highly weathered sands and gravels, bear soils (podsols) which poorly retain nutrients for plant growth and may be either freely draining and droughty, or waterlogged due to an impervious iron pan in the subsoil. This is Hardy's bleak 'Egdon Heath' which seems naturally to grow mainly heather and gorse.

Heathland may appear to be natural on these parent materials, but archaeological evidence strongly suggests that human activity played an important part in creating it. The earliest field monuments in any number on the heathland are burial mounds which date to the Bronze Age. These were usually built on the original ground surface of material dug from a surrounding ditch, and old surfaces are often recognisable

7 The heathland landscape looking north-west from Ballard Head

beneath them. The soils on these have a form that reflects their vegetation and use and, also in this environment, contain pollen from the plants growing nearby. Several such soils have been studied,[9] and in general they suggest that the barrows were built on surfaces which had not yet become fully developed podsols. Podsols develop when vegetation, which can maintain the nutrient levels in the soil (e.g. established mixed woodland), is removed, and the nutrients are leached out, leaving a medium in which only plants tolerant of acid and low nutrient conditions can survive, e.g. heather and gorse. Studies of the buried pollen support this deduction; not long before the barrows were built there was mixed oak woodland nearby, then heathland vegetation replaced it. Several lines of evidence point to late Neolithic, early Bronze Age farming as the human agent of deforestation, which when associated with appropriate climatic conditions, led to the landscape we now see.

A not dissimilar history attaches to the chalk landscape. Apart, perhaps, from the very exposed high downland, this too acquired a covering of open oak woodland after the last Ice Age, which was removed by the earliest farmers in the Neolithic period. In this case, deforestation led to the loss of richer soil cover and to the formation of very thin rendzina soils seen today, which are dominated by a single nutrient: calcium. Under continuous grazing, particularly by sheep, these soils support a short turf containing a very diverse flora of grasses and herbs, which are valued today as 'natural' downland. If left alone this rapidly reverts to scrub and woodland; paradoxically, it too is an artificial landscape which needs to be managed if it is to remain 'natural'.

Unlike the heathland, which was opened up relatively late and abandoned soon after, the chalk downs were marked by much of the ebb and flow of prehistoric and later activity. They accumulated traces of domestic, agricultural and ritual practices. These chalk landscapes were once much richer archaeological resources than the heathlands, but only thin soils clothed their slight banks and mounds and, lightly buried their ditches and pits, soils which offer little protection from the plough. Much concern is expressed about the loss of ecologically precious heathland to mineral working, waste disposal and housing development, but the loss of chalk downland under the plough has been relatively unlamented. In the second half of the twentieth century, incentives were given to farmers to plough up downland and convert it to cereal production. This resulted in the destruction of most of the downland that had been maintained under sheep grazing since prehistoric times. Whilst there had been earlier assaults by the plough, their archaeological impact was small, because early ploughs did not penetrate much beneath the topsoil. Ploughs of today dig deep, biting into archaeological evidence and destroying it.

A good example of this process in action, and an attempt to reverse it, can be seen on the slopes to the north. If the land is bare and recently ploughed, the fields to the north will almost certainly appear a very pale brown, almost white. This is due to the thinness of the topsoil, which has been dispersed amongst the chalk rubble dug up by the plough, washed down the slope, or blown away. (Much artificial fertiliser is added to grow crops in these conditions, to compensate for this loss of top soil.) To the north-east and in the foreground there is downland, of a sort. This represents an attempt by the National Trust to encourage the conversion of arable land back into traditional downland turf. (At the time of writing, its immaturity could be seen by the scatter of stones on the surface, which the action of earthworms would have buried on historic downland.) Restoration may succeed from an ecological perspective, but from an archaeological point of view, it is too late.

So, this is not a landscape one would see if 'nature' alone had produced it. It is the result of an interaction between climate, rocks, soils and human management. In very few places along the Heritage Coast, probably none landward of the cliff-edge, can landscapes be found which do not contain a human agent in their development. Perhaps one should talk of 'historic', rather than 'natural' landscapes when wishing to emphasise the value of their antiquity and absence of recent human interference.

This is the best view of the part of the Dorset coast beyond Shell Bay, and a good place to introduce a topic – aspects which will be encountered directly later: Iron Age and Romano-British industry. For many today, a mention of Poole will invoke a thought of pottery, and large-scale exploitation of the famous ball-clays that are a component of the Tertiary deposits. Pottery making on a large scale in this area has an early history, which may be less well known. During the later Iron Age, settlements around the shores of Poole Harbour concentrated on producing distinctive pottery, Black burnished ware, fired in small clamp kilns. This industry intensified dramatically in the Romano-British period, when the products were transported widely in response to increasing market activity. Linked with this was the exploitation of other raw materials offered by the region, particularly Purbeck limestone and Kimmeridge shale in domestic and ornamental use, and sea-water in the extraction of salt. Good examples of carefully conducted and thoroughly analysed excavations of industrial sites of this period at Ower and Norden north-east of Corfe Castle have been published,[10] and current excavations at the very important multi-period site at Bestwall Quarry, Wareham, promise to substantially increase knowledge of early pottery production.[11]

On a clear day Hengistbury Head, the eastern limit of the Dorset Coast, can be seen from here. It has important archaeological sites of several periods, including a camping place of Upper Palaeolithic hunters, probably the earliest site on the Dorset coast. But it may be best known for its Iron Age defences, which isolate the peninsula from the mainland. Hengistbury was of great importance at this time for its function as a port through which goods were exchanged with Continental Europe.[12]

FROM BALLARD DOWN TO DURLSTON HEAD

From here, the coast path crosses Swanage. Where settlement ends at Peveril Point, there are several concrete structures, one beneath the National Coastwatch station. Their cavernous appearance is reminiscent of the gun emplacement seen at Studland and, these too are the sites of coastal defence guns. The western-most has associated support and observation structures and a fragment of a gun traverse on the edge of a concrete platform to its east.

The rocks which outcrop at Peveril Point and to its south (SZ 041787 to 036782) are worth examining, because this is the only exposure of the Purbeck Beds which can be studied before the archaeological evidence of their quarrying for useful building stones is encountered. Notice how the beds of massive cream or greyish limestone which are valuable as building and sculptural stone alternate with beds of material which the quarryman treats as waste. This natural pattern and the orientation of the beds places constraints on quarrying. It will be seen later that these are reflected in the archaeological evidence for the activity.

The rock which forms part of the ledge stretching out to sea from Peveril Point is Purbeck marble. A close examination where it crosses the shore beneath the eastern-most gun emplacement will show small helical shells of a freshwater mollusc set in a fine cement, but will not reveal the beauty of this rock when polished. This property caught the imagination of medieval masons and the rock was widely used in decorating ecclesiastical buildings. It was first noticed by stone masons not long after the Roman Conquest. Architectural mouldings, floor or wall tiles and inscriptions made of Purbeck marble, are found at several civil and military sites in contexts as early as the mid-first century AD.[13] This early date may suggest that the Roman Army were involved in the exploitation of this rock and it is possible that this resulted from their 'prospecting'. If this speculation is correct, then it is also possible that their attention was attracted by this outcrop or by the only other at Worbarrow Bay. There is no archaeological evidence directly related to the use of these rocks at this location, but excavation of a workshop site at Norden near Corfe Castle[14] has revealed fascinating details of the processing of Purbeck marble in the Romano-British period.

Follow the coast path towards Durlston, but instead of keeping to the coast, make for the Durlston Country Park Centre (which is built on the site of a Second World War Oboe[15] station), to the west of which there is an interesting archaeological landscape.

FROM DURLSTON HEAD TO EMMETT'S HILL

A feature which is often (but not infallibly) helpful in distinguishing artificial from natural features of the landscape, is geometrical regularity and symmetry: those with a human cause are usually more regular than those caused by natural processes. An example of this is to be seen in the fields to the north of the path, west of the Country Park Centre, where there a regular series of long low ridges running north-south. Similar to those seen at Studland, these are the remains of strip fields within the medieval open-field agricultural landscape of Swanage and Herston. Other examples will be seen with increasing clarity towards Winspit, where their formation and use will be discussed.

Cross the head of the valley running down to the lighthouse, turn south at the first wall, and make for the top of the hill. The ridge and slope to the south are formed by the Purbeck beds and they are covered by mounds and hollows which disturb the general profile of the landscape. What caused them?

This is a very turbulent landscape and regularity will not help here in distinguishing an artificial from a natural cause. The problem is easier to study if attention is focused on one of the elements that make up a picture which may be overwhelmingly complicated as a whole. Find a mound where erosion by farm stock and walkers have exposed its contents. Notice the roughly broken, angular, randomly orientated limestone pieces. This suggests that it was made from material haphazardly thrown together, which had not had time to weather on the surface. In some cases there will be a hollow beside the mound, from which the material appears to have come. Depressions of similar dimensions, 'sink holes' or 'dolines', can form in limestone by natural solution processes, but their form is generally more regular and they are not associated with mounds of spoil. On the level ground at least, the only plausible source of energy for this displacement is human. This hummocky surface is not the result of natural processes.

In some of the hollows, outcrops of limestone can be seen, most likely on the up-slope sides. The acquisition of this material was the motive for expending energy disturbing the ground. The hollows are the remains of Purbeck Stone quarries; the mounds are heaps of waste discarded in the quest for valuable stone. This is an industrial landscape: a confusion of quarrying activity over a long period. The mounds have been left alone for long enough to acquire a thin covering of soil, and the quarries are overgrown with scrub. There has been no quarrying here for many years.

Most of the evidence in this location seems to suggest that open cast quarrying was the main method of extraction, which would require less effort if good stone was readily available near the surface. But this is misleading: underground mines were much used to follow the beds of valuable stone, particularly when surface outcrops had been removed. Some of the hollows may be the blocked entrances of these. *Colour plate 3* is a view eastwards across this quarry-pocked landscape from SZ026771. In the foreground is a quarry pit; there is the restored entrance to a stone mine in the middle distance with whim (windlass) and quarr cart – the device with which stone was hauled to the surface *(colour plate 4)*. Other evidence of stone mining can be seen in the cliff near the lighthouse, but this form of extraction can be better studied further west at Seacombe and Winspit.

Continue due west on the top of the ridge and cross the next wall. After 50m, look carefully for more regularity amongst the strewn quarry spoil. At SZ025771 there are traces of a roughly rectangular stone-work enclosure, breaking through the turf. Its long axis is orientated east-west and there is a slight ditch at each end *(colour plate 5)*. At the western end some thin slabs of limestone, set on edge, protrude through the turf *(fore-ground of colour plate 5)*. They look like rough curb stones. Some are aligned with the enclosure, some oblique to it, and their orientations might suggest more than one phase of construction. Inside, there is a smaller slightly embanked enclosure. A few metres to the south, in a terrace cut into the scarp slope just beneath the crest of the ridge (possibly a disused quarry hollow), a few courses of dry stone walling indicate the remains of smaller enclosures *(8)*, and remains of similar enclosures, all of un-dressed dry stone, can be seen to the north.

Given the predominance of quarrying here, the possibility that these were quarry buildings is the first interpretation to consider. Buildings

8 The signal station buildings, Durlston

are commonly associated with quarries, often in the form of three-sided shelters to protect quarrymen from the elements whilst dressing stone. These were often of simple dry stone construction. Some of the features of this site are therefore consistent with quarry buildings. But early quarry buildings tend to be dispersed, and to lack the regularity of arrangement at this site.

The most compelling argument against an origin in quarrying relies on a feature on the north side of the site. Here, heading down the slope from the west end of the main enclosure, is a well made stone path *(9)* which leads to the remains of a short flight of steps, revetted either side with dry stone walls, on the steepest part of the slope *(10)*. Because the path overlies earlier quarry workings and is avoided by later ones, the character of its masonry and its position all suggest an approach to the enclosure site rather than a quarry track or later enhancement of a footpath.

This is probably as far as inference in the field can go, but the site has been identified[16] as the remains of a signalling station shown on the 1811 Ordnance Survey map. This is one of a series of coastal signalling stations set up in the late eighteenth century as an early warning system in response to the threat of invasion by France. These stations were equipped with means of symbolic signalling using flags and other devices,

9 *top* The signal station path, Durlston

10 *above* The signal station steps, Durlston

11 Nine Barrow (Ailwood) Down, from Durlston

12 Barrows on Ailwood Down: the long barrow is to the left of three round barrows

and manned by the Sea Fencibles.[17] The signalling tower is presumed to be in the central enclosure. Among the other stations in the series was one on Ballard Down, the remains of which might be identified with the earthwork referred to earlier. Both appear to have been closed in 1814. Traces of others will be seen at White Nothe and Golden Cap.

Continuing westwards from Round Down, the path is high enough at SZ009771 for the chalk ridge to the north to be seen *(11)*; there is a group of round mounds on its crest. The name of the ridge, Nine Barrow Down, indicates that these are burial mounds of the early Bronze Age, built between 2000 and 1500 BC. This setting is characteristic of round barrow groups on the Chalk in southern Britain. The contents and forms of Bronze Age barrows will be considered later.

Closer examination of this group would show that one of the mounds is not actually round: it is an elongated oval *(12)*. This shape strongly suggests that it is earlier than the others; long barrows are common in the early Neolithic. Excavation has not tested the point, but if this barrow is Neolithic, it is the only field monument in this area which records the presence of people, probably cereal farming, perhaps earlier than 3000 BC.[18]

The official coast path to the south focuses attention on the archaeology of the cliff-edge, and from Anvil Point to Winspit this is an archaeology of caves and ledges. Whilst some of these can be explained by the action of the sea, those above sea level cannot, and they are far too fresh to have been made by higher sea levels of an interglacial many tens of millennia ago. The rocks forming the cliff belong to the Portland beds, which contain excellent building stones. Given the intense industrial activity stimulated by the Purbeck limestone already seen, association of these cliff features with quarrying will be readily made.

The evidence shows how quarrying methods were adapted to topography and situation. The Portland beds lie almost horizontally here, and outcrop at the cliff and in the mouths of valleys such as Seacombe and Winspit. Initial extraction from the cliff outcrops led to the creation of ledges and, from the valley mouth, outcrops led automatically to the creation of adits following the building stones. In time, both often broadened into 'galleries' supported at intervals by stone pillars. Before the availability of effective and economical road transport, these coastal quarries were favourably placed to use maritime transport, stone being loaded directly, and hazardously, into boats.

Features of the industrial archaeology of the cliff quarries can be examined at various points along the path, such as at Dancing Ledge (where a rectangular basin in the ledge might defy explanation: it was made as a tide-filled swimming pool for a local private school) but access is always more or less dangerous, and this is better left until Winspit.

At Seacombe, it is worth examining the rusting steel dome on the eastern side of the valley, just above the cliff path at SY996767 *(colour plate 6)*. The dome is pierced by two hatches and covers a small underground chamber, which is accessed by a narrow cutting lined with steel plate. When it contained less rubble, there would have been just enough room to accommodate one person. Inside, the rollers which permitted it to be rotated can be seen, as can struts to support a weapon. Another Second World War artefact, this is type of pillbox known as an Alan-Williams turret. It may have been protecting the building in the valley below. The materials and form of the latter suggest that it is of the same date, but it is not possible to infer a function from the field evidence *(13)*.

The Path climbs the west side of the valley and joins a grass-covered track. Beside the track the quarried blocks of stone are well worth examining. Some carry traces of trapeze-shaped indentations chiselled into their edges. These are the sides of pits which were cut in a line along which the quarryman wanted the stone to split.[19] Wedges were driven into the pits to split the stone. Other blocks carry drilled holes which were used instead of chiselled pits, in the splitting of stone when

13 The foundations of a probable Second World War building, Seacombe

14 Extracted stone, Seacombe: chiselled wedge pit (1), drilled hole, roughly dressed face (3)

compressed air drills became available. Most blocks also carry tooling marks acquired in rough dressing to shape *(14)*.

The track curves westwards and becomes a terrace which can be traced to an open cast quarry. On its south side there is a concrete pad and the quarry edge beside it is free from spoil. This suggests the location of a crane for lifting extracted stone. It is reasonable to infer that it was a steam crane, as the soil around the pad contains coal and cinders.

The safest access to the cliff quarry environment is at Winspit, where quarries to the east and west of the inlet can be examined; *but extreme caution is necessary when approaching the cliff-edge and the quarry faces, and the galleries themselves should not be entered.* From the outside a good impression of the method of supporting the roofs can be gained. Sometimes pillars of stone were left *in situ*; alternatively they were constructed from large blocks of stone. On the upper ledge at East Winspit, traces of the holes for the posts of wooden cranes used for lowering stone to the lower ledge or directly into boats can be found *(15)*. Other details are worth looking for near the cliff-edge if the tide is not too high, such as rut-ways, along which stone was hauled in carts for shipment *(16)*.

29

15 *Opposite above* Cliff crane post holes, East Winspit

16 *Opposite below* Rut-ways, lower ledge, Winspit

17 *Above* Smithy, West Winspit

At West Winspit there are also the remains of buildings and machinery hold-fasts, which were probably in use when the quarries closed in the middle of the twentieth century. The eastern-most contains a chimney and brick fireplace *(17)*. Confronted with substantial hearths, archaeologists are inclined to speculate about their symbolism and status of their owners, but it is worth considering functional explanations before invoking social or ideological ones, and there is a good functional reason to have a substantial hearth in a quarry. The clue to that function is the stone which lies between the hearth and the door. It has the impression of the foot of an anvil in the mortar on its surface. This strongly suggests the building was a smithy; the hearth was a blacksmith's forge. Quarrymen rapidly blunt their steel tools working stone. The blacksmith would have heated them in the forge, shaped new cutting edges on the anvil, sharpened them, and finally hardened and tempered them by reheating and quenching. Specialist knowledge[20] is needed to interpret most of the other structures, but there is a clue which suggests a function for one of the structures at the western end. This is a cone of light brown sand spreading out to the south (to the right of the brick plinth in the foreground of *Figure 18*), which seems to have flowed down a channel to the east of the floor covering a sump with two manhole covers. A possible explanation is that the sand was used as an abrasive in stone cutting, and therefore that one of these structures supported a stone saw.

18 A building possibly associated with stone sawing, Winspit

It is worth noting the differential weathering in the brickwork of these buildings.[21] One wall shows two very different degrees of weathering damage. If two phases of building had seemed to be associated with this difference, it would have been reasonable to suppose the most weathered to be the older. But there is a single phase of building and the difference in weathering is due to the difference in the resistance of the bricks. Later[22] an argument about age will be based on the weathering of concrete; at that point it would be as well to remember this cautionary example.

On both sides of the Winspit valley are terraces, much more obvious than those noted at Studland and Durlston. They are much longer than they are wide, mostly running parallel with the contours of the slope *(colour plate 7)*. These are the remains of medieval arable farming, and probably result from ploughing technology that was different from the one which produced the smaller, nearly square fields of the Romano-British period and earlier, to be discussed at Hounstout. These later fields were cultivated with a plough which had a mould board, a device enabling it to turn over a furrow in the manner of ploughs used today. Breaking up and inverting the soil with this plough could be achieved in a single action, and, as it was drawn by a team of oxen, it would have been expedient to turn it as infrequently as possible. This practice would have tended to produce long narrow fields, which on steep slopes like these tend to be along contours, which would have maximised the amount of level ploughing. They are termed 'strip lynchets'. These fields were probably established in the twelfth or thirteenth century when increasing population was putting intense pressure on land for food production. Medieval farmers were unable to increase crop yield on the land under cultivation so more land had to go under the plough. On the heavier lands to the west this led to accelerated clearing of woodland; in this area it led to the exploitation of land that was very hard to work. As ploughing continued over a long period, soil creeping and washing down the slope from the higher boundary of each strip to accumulate at the lower boundary would have gradually produced these pronounced steps etched so deeply into the hillside that they are still respected when the slopes are cultivated today. On the steeper slopes they often reverted to uncultivated pasture when population declined in the fourteenth century and the farming of sheep became dominant, and thus escaped later destruction. In the medieval period, in this region, unenclosed strips were often grouped into a small number of

19 Chain Home Low radar station, St Aldhelm's Head

large fields surrounding the settlement with open areas of common grazing beyond. Strips were held and cultivated by individuals, but the system was managed 'in common'.[23] The post-medieval survival of the open field holdings of Worth Matravers and their subsequent enclosure have been the subject of a recent study.[24]

As the path levels towards St Aldhelm's Head, it skirts the remains of a quarry terrace (SY963754) which is easily accessible and contains the remains of several buildings well worth examining. Two are represented by floors only, but the central building has standing walls *(19)*. Notice that these are made from bonded roughly dressed limestone, and have earth banks built up against their outer walls. Despite the lack of Second World War concrete (though there is some nearby in the flight of steps giving access to the ledge from the west), the banks are unmistakably Second World War blast proofing. This building housed a Second World War low-level (Chain Home Low) radar which was designed to locate aircraft flying below the beam of the main early warning system (Chain Home). A contemporary photograph shows the aerial for transmitting the radar pulse and receiving the echo to have been on the roof of the brick-lined room at the east.[25] The building would have held the plotting equipment, the transmitter and receiver and the generator which supplied electrical power. There is a direct entrance on the south side, wide enough to permit the installation of heavy equipment – traces of the tarmacadam track can be seen leading to this from the east. The crew entrance on the north side is narrower and indirect. The crew accommodation was sited to the east of this block and survives as a rectangular concrete floor with a flight of steps to an entrance at the eastern end. Internal divisions are visible.

On the cliff-edge to the south-west of the main site is the floor of a small square building. This is a survival of activity at this site by the Telecommunications Research Establishment (TRE) which did work of the highest importance in the development of radar between 1940 and 1942. This hut is impossible to interpret from the field evidence, beyond a description of its concrete floor, grey-brick cavity wall with slate damp course and entrance porch to the north; primary documentary evidence about this episode does not appear to contain the level of detail to take this further. For sites within living memory, however, personal testimony is potentially of great value if those who can remember them can be interviewed. This site well illustrates the point. One of the TRE scientists testified that he had worked in this hut, or its wooden predecessor, doing original measurements on the properties of aerials being designed for use in low-level radar detection, which at the time were barely understood.[26]

The sculpture beside the path just to the east of the National Coastwatch Lookout commemorates this work. Its interlaced skeletal parabolas echo the shape of the aerial which was designed by Sir Bernard Lovell (a member of the TRE research team, and later the pioneer radio astronomer who built the Jodrell Bank radio telescope) to transmit and receive radar signals of very short wavelength. The significance of this will be considered at Hounstout, from where the former location of the TRE sites can better be seen.

The path westwards passes four concrete plinths, probably the base of a Second World War communications mast. To the north is the eleventh century St Aldhelm's chapel, which has some interesting, but so far unexamined, earthworks enclosing it. On a clear day, the view of the coast sweeping west to Portland Bill is breathtaking. The drab grey rocks forming the lower lying areas are Kimmeridge clay; they are capped by warmer buffs of Portland beds at Hounstout *(20, 1)* and Gad Cliff *(20, 2)*. In the distance, the brilliant white is the chalk at Bindon Hill *(20, 3)*

20 The coast west from St Aldhelm's Head: Hounstout (1), Gad Cliff (2), Bindon Hill (3), White Nothe (4)

21 The location of an Iron Age – Romano-British site (1), St Aldhelm's Head

and White Nothe *(20, 4)*. To the north-east, beyond the quarry, is the location of the Iron Age – Romano-British site *(21, 1)* which will be described below.

Notice the pile of grey brick and concrete on the extreme edge of the cliff. *Take great care as there is a sheer drop at this point.* This is all that remains of a Second World War building which was demolished; most of it bulldozed over the cliff. It is a reminder of the widespread 'clean-up' (i.e. destruction) of wartime heritage which occurred because it was thought aesthetically displeasing, or dangerous and, not interesting enough to warrant preservation. Ironically, at the time of writing, English Heritage are engaged in an exercise to schedule the best of what little is left of this important record to ensure its indefinite protection.

At the point where the path descends steeply into Pier Bottom, look north-east up the valley for traces of small square-like earthworks. These are prehistoric fields, like those mentioned at Handfast Point, usually called 'celtic fields' (though their origins can be much earlier than the Iron Age which gave rise to the name). They result from a different method of ploughing to that which produced the medieval strip lynchets seen at Winspit – a technique which will be discussed later.

It will be assumed that the marked coast path, which climbs steeply to Emmett's Hill, will be followed. This route is, in any case, archaeologically more interesting than the unofficial scramble via Chapman's Pool.

View Point: Emmett's Hill
From the top of the steps, the north-facing slope of Pier Bottom valley can be seen, where traces of celtic fields are clearer *(22, 1)*. As the crest of the slope is gained, the landscape opens to the east and the occupation site probably associated with them which was mentioned earlier

22 Celtic fields (1) and Bronze Age barrow (2), Pier Bottom valley

(21, 1) comes into view beyond the quarry. The site (SY966761) is likely to be typical of the mixed farming settlements of the Iron Age and Romano-British period found on all the easily cultivated soils on the Jurassic limestone hills in the area. One feature of the site, marked by a pile of stones, is a storage pit of particular interest. It was found in 1982 when ploughing broke through limestone capping to reveal an almost empty, barrel-shaped cavity, more than a metre in diameter, at least 3m deep, cut into the soft sediments which overlie the Portland limestone at this point, and finished off with corbelled courses of dry stone walling at the top. Pits of this general type, the primary purpose of which was the storage of grain, are common on Iron Age settlements in lowland Britain. Frequently they were filled with rubbish, or more interesting 'votive' deposits, when their storage function ceased (possibly because they became contaminated) but this one was almost empty, presumably because it was abandoned with cereal grain in it, which decayed leaving a void. On first opening the sides of the pit bore, with striking clarity, the marks of an axe-like tool which was used to cut them.[27]

South-west of this site at SY 963759 *(22, 2)* is a round barrow which was opened in the nineteenth century to reveal burials and grave goods of Bronze Age date, but also a substantial quantity of Romano-British material, probably of domestic origin, which is likely to be associated with the occupation site.

The most recent excavation of a similar site in the vicinity was at Compact Farm, where intermittent occupation from the early Iron Age to the late Romano-British period was represented by a number of buildings, the early ones round in plan, the latest rectangular and containing a corn drier.[28] The excavation report also discusses economic and ritual aspects of the site which are relevant to others mentioned later. It is an excellent example of the detail that can be achieved by a modest excavation conducted to very high standards.

Beside the path where it levels out and turns slightly to the north, there is another Bronze Age burial mound. It is right on the cliff-edge and somewhat disturbed, partly by cliff erosion.

Opening to the north is Kingston Down, a Portland stone promontory separated from Emmett's Hill and Hounstout by valleys from Kingston, Hill Bottom and Worth Matravers, which drain into Chapman's Pool. This is the site of the best preserved Iron Age – Romano-British farming landscape on the whole of the Dorset

23 Kingston Down from Emmett's Hill: prehistoric trackway (1), and other tracks (2) and (3)

Heritage coast. The view of the earthworks on the south-eastern flank improve as the coast path is followed northwards and are best studied late in the day when the sun is low in the west. (Early morning visitors are best served by the view from Hounstout.) From the coast path stone marked 'Hill Bottom ¾' it is possible to make out corners of celtic field boundaries on the top of the hill, though these are much better seen from Hounstout. There are also three linear features, one descending from the fields on top of the hill towards the north-east *(23, 1)*, and two ascending to meet it from different points lower down the hill to the south-west *(23, 2 and 3)*; they look like long disused footpaths. The uppermost has been shown to be contemporary with the settlement,[29] and the others may be, or they may be later, but still of some antiquity. The obvious rectangular feature in the middle of the facing slope is just possibly an old quarry, but it is more likely to be a landslip scar, as the whole of the slope below its top edge appears to be involved in the disturbance. These slopes are rather unstable, as can been seen from the scars of other slips nearby, but they are usually crescent shaped rather than rectilinear, so there is room for doubt. If this is a landslide, it cut through the higher path, and therefore is later than the path. If it is a quarry, the path could be seen as associated with it, possibly for transporting stone to the top of the hill.

FROM EMMETT'S HILL TO HOUNSTOUT

Descending from Renscombe Farm into the Hill Bottom valley, the terrace which can be seen to the north of the road at SY963778 is the course of an old coach road to Encombe House on the far side of Hounstout. Beyond the hamlet, the metalled track coincides with this old road, until it crosses an embankment pierced by a beautifully constructed culvert. Note the remains of a sheep-wash in the stream just to the north. The coast path continues to follow the old road as it turns south and heads for a cutting in the cliff at the foot of Hounstout at SY953772; its course is indicated by arrows in *Figure 24*. Here it has been ploughed out, but under favourable conditions can be seen as a cropmark. It will be encountered again on the western slope of Hounstout.

24 Hounstout from Emmett's Hill: the arrows mark the path of the old coach road from Encombe House

View Point: Hounstout

The landscape from north-east to south-east is dominated by the limestone plateaux of Kingston Down, Emmett's Hill and St Aldhelm's Head, and the almost dry valleys long ago cut down through the Portland series to the Kimmeridge clay, which forms the floor of the hummocky plateau in the foreground and Chapman's Pool bay.

At the northern end of Emmett's Hill are the buildings of Renscombe Farm. To the east and south of this farm, some of the most important scientific and engineering work of the Second World War was undertaken in the greatest secrecy. This was where the Telecommunications Research Establishment of the Air Ministry employed the team of 'boffins' and support staff who were developing radar. Their work covered a wide range of devices and techniques, but perhaps their most significant contribution during their occupation of this site between 1940 and 1942, was the creation of a powerful short-wave radar small enough to be flown in aircraft, and with high enough resolution to enable crews to locate enemy aircraft at night. Later developments of this equipment during the war would be used to detect submarines, to direct gunnery and to identify land targets for bombing. The key to these developments was the invention by two scientists at Birmingham University of an efficient generator of electromagnetic radiation with a wavelength of a few centimetres. The device was called the cavity magnetron, and it was on the hilltop above Chapman's Pool that the magnetron was first incorporated in a practical radar transmitter.[30]

After the war, this site became part of a network of radio navigation transmitters known as Gee stations. It was operated until the 1960s. The site was then almost completely demolished, and now only a couple of buildings remain. However, after a prolonged dry spell, a rectangular cropmark can be seen draped over the shoulder of the slope to the west of Renscombe Farm *(25, 1)*. This cropmark results from the grass being unable to obtain enough moisture from the very thin soil to remain green. Inspection shows that this thin soil lies over a trench containing very rusty coiled barbed wire.

The ridge towards the north-east is Kingston Down. On the facing slope the rectangular outlines of a system of fields belonging to a farming settlement on the hilltop can be seen *(26)*. This was almost certainly occupied during the Iron Age, may have had its origins earlier still and was probably still in use in the Romano-British period. It is one

25 Emmett's Hill from Hounstout: the site of the Second World War Telecommunications Research Establishment crop mark (1)

26 Kingston Down prehistoric farm, from Hounstout

of the best preserved farms of this date in the area and, a walk to the top of the hill would reveal the remains of walls outlining 'celtic fields', a trackway leading off to the east,[31] a 'flask-shaped' enclosure, round house sites and storage pits. The farm probably supported an extended family who grew primitive wheat and barley and raised sheep and cattle.[32] Cultivation over many generations cut deep into the subsoil making the fields on the slopes particularly prominent, where soil has gradually moved downhill creating 'lynchets' at the top and the bottom of each field. These fields are small and almost square, in contrast to the later elongated strip lynchets at Winspit. This shape is likely to result from the use of a more primitive method for breaking up the soil and creating a tilth. It is probable that these farmers used an ard for this purpose, a kind of ox-drawn hoe, which could cut a groove in the topsoil, but could not turn over the furrow burying the turf as the later mould-board ploughs could. From the study of marks left in the subsoil of fields of this period elsewhere, it seems that the ard was used in a series of passes in one direction and then again in another series perpendicular to the first. It is generally thought that a rational application of this 'cross-ploughing' on sloping ground would tend to create equi-dimensional fields engraved into the surface in the manner seen here. Stones, probably cleared from the cultivated areas, form low 'walls' on their margins. Quite elaborate systems of land management existed in several parts of the country, at least by the later Bronze Age and, some areas may well have been sub-divided into square-like fields from the start, and not simply to have resulted from a method of cultivation. There are indications that the Kingston Down field system was laid out deliberately within large rectilinear divisions of the area defined by dry stone walls. Indeed, it has been suggested that in these boundaries on the hilltop can be seen the division of land between two farms.[33] These indications, and the distribution of surface finds, suggests that by the Iron Age, the southern slopes of the Isle of Purbeck were densely settled.

Two other features are visible in this view of Emmett's Hill. Traces of trackways, probably of some antiquity, lead down towards Chapman's Pool, and the numerous hollows along the crest of the ridge are small quarries of unknown date. They may be ancient, but they may be associated with the building of enclosure walls in the eighteenth and nineteenth centuries. Similar quarry pits exist on almost every site in the area capable of yielding casual stone.

27 Swyre Head (1) and Eldon's Seat prehistoric site (2), from Hounstout

Below on the shore there are the remains of a small square building with mortared rough stone walls. This is known locally as 'the Powder House' and it would be a reasonable guess to link it with the early years of coastguard service, perhaps in the later eighteenth century, when they would have patrolled the shore in an effort to detect the running of contraband.

Turning to the west, the Portland limestone ridge curves gently around the northern boundary of the Encombe valley to terminate in another headland, Swyre Head *(27, 1)*, which is surmounted by a large mound capped with a stone platform. The platform is a nineteenth-century addition, and at that time the mound may have been enlarged, but it is likely that beneath it there is a Bronze Age burial mound in this prominent location. Another, much denuded, lies to its north-east.

The plateau that forms the Encombe valley floor and the cliffs stretching west towards Kimmeridge, is Kimmeridge clay. This generally provides rather heavy ill-drained soils which one might expect early farmers to have avoided; but they did not. On the gentle east-facing slope at the foot of Swyre Head *(27, 2)* lies the prehistoric farmstead known as Eldon's Seat – the name is taken from the massive stone seat set on the ridge above by Lord Eldon in 1835. The most thorough excavations of this site (at SY940775) were undertaken in the early 1960s.[34] These showed that the occupation of this small mixed farmstead began at the end of the Bronze Age or in the earliest phase of the Iron Age, probably earlier than 600 BC, and continued intermittently until the second century AD. During this time the lynchet, which can still be seen under appropriate conditions running north–south across the site, was growing as a result of cultivation of fields further up the slope to the west. Over the generations this sometimes encroached on the farm buildings; at other times, replacement buildings were dug into the lynchet. An additional activity on the site was the working of bituminous Kimmeridge shale to make decorative objects such as bracelets – a topic which will be developed below.

FROM HOUNSTOUT TO CLAVEL TOWER

Near the foot of the steep slope descending west from Hounstout is a cutting on the cliff-edge, complementary to that seen on the eastern slope, which marks the course of the old coach road once connecting Encombe House with Worth Matravers and Swanage. This road included a spectacular cliff section which traversed the Kimmeridge clay bench (the Half-cliff), some 80m above the sea beneath Hounstout. Erosion and landslips have carried this section of the road away, leaving occasional traces of a terrace edged with massive rough limestone slabs in the brambles below, and these cuttings on the east and west slopes which now lead to a sheer drop. From Swyre Head the western cutting can be seen *(28, 1)* below traces of celtic fields at least 2,000 years older than the road. These once capped hills above and are further evidence of the intensity of agricultural activity towards the end of the prehistoric period.

At the foot of the hill there is a stream which meets the sea in a waterfall cascading from a small promontory. This is Freshwater Steps, but the steps which used to descend the cliff here have long since been destroyed by cliff erosion and their remains are part of the archaeological record. Traces of the stone blocks at the base can be seen on the beach. *(Take care!)* The stone wall and pillars terminating the culvert which carries the stream under the footpath bear traces of the

28 Hounstout from Swyre Head: old coach road cutting

depredations of the Second World War; the stumps are all that remain of wrought iron railings which are believed to have been removed in the campaign to supplement dwindling metal stocks.

There is an interesting fragment of industrial archaeology buried in undergrowth just to the north of the path at this point, though it is on private property and not accessible to the public. A flight of stone steps, surrounded by the remains of a wrought iron fence and gate, leads to a circular, subterranean room with a domed stone roof. In the centre of the floor is a hand operated water pump which once gathered seawater from an inlet built into the seabed beyond the waterfall and delivered it to a bath at Encombe House, a kilometre or so inland. This site, along with the adventurous coach road mentioned above, and also much domestic building of the highest quality on the Encombe Estate, symbolises the wealth and imagination of the Scott family in the nineteenth century.

The path climbs past the ridge marked by Eldon's Seat then descends to a plateau which maintains this height until it reaches Kimmeridge

29 The prehistoric site near Ropelake Head

Bay. The path is now on Kimmeridge clay which the cliff exposures show to comprise soft dark grey clays interrupted rhythmically with harder beds including limestone. Amongst these harder beds, there are a small number of dense black shales which can be polished, and which burn with a pungent smell (explaining its local name Kimmeridge coal). These properties derive from its high content of bitumen and also account for the importance of the Kimmeridge clay in the archaeological record, particularly in the Iron Age and Romano-British periods, and again in the sixteenth, seventeenth and nineteenth centuries.

Amongst the domestic pottery and animal bones at the prehistoric farmstead site near Eldon's Seat, which make up most of the finds on farms of the period, was evidence that bituminous Kimmeridge shale was being worked with iron and flint tools into rings large enough to be bracelets. Further west on the footpath, at SY932776, there is a site, the excavation of which has helped to improve the understanding of shale working. *Figure 29,* taken from the coast path marker inscribed 'Kimmeridge 1½, Chapman's Pool 2¾', shows its location (1).

The excavation, which took place in the 1970s,[35] revealed evidence of occupation including dwellings which were round in the early Iron Age and rectangular in the Romano-British period, echoing the sequence seen at Compact Farm; occupation was continuous in the immediate vicinity for at least 600 years. During the Iron Age rough discs of shale were hand-fashioned; in the Romano-British period a lathe of some kind was used. Precisely circular waste discs, left when the ring has been cut away from its outside, were found bearing chucking and centring marks which could only result from the use of a machine of this kind. A distinctive set of flint tools appears to have been used in conjunction with the lathe. This site is fairly typical of the Iron Age and Romano-British farmsteads in the Isle of Purbeck, and evidence for shale working is found on many of these. At a few sites, trays, bowls and even table or chair legs were made; for a time, on some sites, production seems to have reached an industrial scale.

Where badgers are continuing to disturb the site on the cliff-edge, waste pieces of shale, flints and pottery are often visible on the surface. *Figure 30* shows an example of surface finds, left: animal bone, above centre: briquetage,[36] below centre: piece of rough-out for a shale armlet, right: Iron Age pottery. Occasionally erosion exposes cliff sections which typically show layers of broken stone containing pottery, flint, animal bones and shellfish: limpet and oyster are common. *Do not attempt to disturb this site: neither the badgers nor the archaeology! Look with great care; the cliff is very unstable; these locations are very dangerous.*

30 Artefacts from the prehistoric site near Ropelake Head. See text for identification

31 Railway lines, Clavel's Hard

At SY920777 there is a ledge some 30m wide below the cliff top, which is the result of a much later and much more intensive extraction of bituminous Kimmeridge shale *(colour plate 8)*. It is the remains of cliff quarrying and associated addits constructed in the nineteenth century to extract the material for the industrial exploitation of the chemical rather than the physical properties of the material. When it was in use, there was an extensive system of underground working supplying tens of thousands of tons of shale per year as feedstock to distillation plants at distant locations, which produced gases, oils and waxes, and by-products such as varnish and fertilizer. There was even a contract to supply shale to Paris for the same purpose in about 1860.[37] Chemical exploitation of shale also occurred in the sixteenth and seventeenth centuries, evidence for which will be considered at Kimmeridge Bay.

In the context of intensive shale mining, the railway lines which are hanging precariously over the cliff at SY918778 *(31)* might be thought to be the remains of a mineral railway that could have been used to take shale from cliff quarries to Kimmeridge Bay for shipping. This inter-pretation should be treated with caution, as they have also been identi-fied as part of a moving gunnery target laid out to the north-east and used during the Second World War.[38] This extensive system of railway tracks is still shown on the current edition of the 1:25000 Ordnance Survey map, but was demolished about forty years ago.

On the crest of the Cuddle, at SY913783, there is a square, brick-faced pillbox with embrasures to the east, south and west *(32)*. It is surrounded by a fence of concrete posts and a mast base which appear roughly contemporaneous. These latter features are not usually associ-ated with pillboxes, and perhaps relate to its use in connection with the firing range just mentioned.

Towards the north-east the Portland Limestone ridge forms the skyline. In the early morning or late evening, when the light is grazing the south facing slope, it is easy to see a series of broad ridges perpen-dicular to the contour *(32, 1)*. Apart from their relation to the slope, they are similar to the remains of medieval strip cultivation seen at Winspit. Earlier, the form of these fields was explained in terms of the result of maximising the efficiency of ploughing with a mould board plough and team of oxen. Contour strips minimise the frequency of turning at each end of the furrow, and also keep energy spent on hill climbing to a minimum. The long narrow strips seen here provide the first benefit, but obviously not the second. If they were ploughed, and not dug by hand, the plough must have been pulled up and down the slope; what might have compelled this additional expenditure of effort is not obvious. Presumably, down-slope movement of soil has etched the areas disturbed by cultivation into the slope, and left the uncultivated junctions between the strips standing proud.

A little further west, at SY911783, the U-shaped cutting truncated by the cliff-edge is the remains of one of the first system of tramways constructed to move shale from the mines to the bay[39] *(33, 1)*. It ran north-west and around the Hen Cliff below Clavel Tower. Its traces on this slope can be seen from the north-west, where the path skirts the main car park at Kimmeridge Bay.

View Point: Clavel Tower

From Hen Cliff, beside the Clavel Tower (SY909786) there is a good view of Kimmeridge Bay. The building itself, which could have been

32 A pillbox on the Cuddle. Cross–contour strip fields on Smedmore Hill (1)

33 A shale mining tramway cutting on the west slope of the Cuddle

used as a watch tower, was probably intended to be a feature to enhance the landscape: a folly. It was built by the Revd John Clavell (sic) in the early nineteenth century and is now a good example of a conservation problem. The fabric has badly decayed: it is threatened with cliff erosion, and considerable funding would be needed to conserve it. Yet it has acquired an aesthetic claim on a place in this landscape simply by having existed for several generations, and this is strong enough to have motivated a support group willing to contemplate moving it a safe distance inland. It is worth reflecting on the arbitrary way society attaches value to elements of the past. Sometimes disproportionate significance seems to be accorded things which began almost frivolously, sometimes the destruction of the products of generations of the hardest manual labour is hardly noticed; the case of many ancient field systems on the Chalk is a good example of the latter.

Looking northwards across Kimmeridge Bay towards the cottages, at Gaulter Gap where the stream disgorges, there is a concrete pillbox

34 Kimmeridge Bay from Hen Cliff: Second World War pillbox (1) and anti-tank blocks (2), the site of seventeenth-century glass works (3)

35 The shore beneath Hen Cliff: a nineteenth-century pier (1), a seventeenth-century pier and dock (2)

(34, 1), which by now will be familiar as an element in Dorset's Second World War anti-invasion defences. This is standing in this position on the beach as a result of six decades of marine erosion of the soft Kimmeridgian rocks. Just to the right of the pillbox are two anti-tank blocks *(34, 2)*, similar to those seen at Studland.

Below on the shore line *(take great care – the cliff is very unstable)* some of the limestone blocks are arranged in a more regular pattern than those forming the rocky beach in general. The arrangement is roughly rectangular, with the long axis pointing out to sea *(35, 1)*. Such regularity is a strong indication of human agency: wave action produces a more disordered distribution. The structure is the base of a stone jetty built in the nineteenth century to facilitate transport of Kimmeridge shale by sea, which was being intensively mined at that time for distillation as mentioned above. The chemical exploitation of shale was begun in the late sixteenth century by John Clavell, and developed by his son, Sir William, who used shale as a feedstock to produce alum, a chemical used as a fixing agent in the dying of cloth. He also used shale as the fuel to drive these processes and also in a salt extraction works set up in 1610. In addition, he built a pier and dock and traces of these can be seen north of the later pier *(35, 2)*.

No further traces of this activity can be seen from here, but the boat park in the south-east sector of the bay *(34, 3)* occupies the site of a glassworks which Sir William constructed with Abraham Bigo, after his earlier enterprise had been terminated by the holders of the monopoly in the production of alum.

More is known about this site than any of the other industrial enterprises at Kimmeridge and it is the only site to have been excavated to modern rigorous standards.[40] The glass house was built in 1617 and produced good quality drinking vessels. It was sited at Kimmeridge to take advantage of the local 'coal' (i.e. bituminous shale) as fuel, when glass makers were beginning to turn to coal from their traditional fuel, wood. The excavation revealed the lower parts of a furnace in which air was drawn through two underground flues to ventilate a central fire. Glass was melted in crucibles (probably four) placed in the furnace. Studies of the fuel and glass composition suggested that the furnace could have operated at a maximum temperature of $1,350°C$. The crucibles appear to have had a base diameter of about 35cm, were more or less cylindrical, and were about 40cm high. Petrographic and heavy mineral analysis[41] suggested that the material used for the crucibles was ball clay found in the Poole basin, the nearest sources of which would have been Norden, north of Corfe Castle. Additional structures for working and annealing glass were identified. All was enclosed by a stone wall and roofed with shale tiles. There was room in the excavated structures for two glass blowers to work. They produced mostly glass bottles, flasks and beakers, and much smaller proportions of other forms such as wine glasses, jugs and bowls. Some were decorated and some blown into moulds. The glass was green as a result of the sand used in its composition, which was thought likely to have come from the Portland beds to the north of Kimmeridge. The glass works only operated for a short period. It was demolished in 1623 as a result of a court action brought by the monopoly holder against Sir William for selling his glass in London, in breach of a restriction in his licence which permitted him to sell his glass only in Dorset, Devon, Cornwall, Hampshire and Wiltshire.

FROM KIMMERIDGE TO GAD CLIFF

From the foot of Hen Cliff where the path crosses the valley (note the Second World War 'dragon's teeth'), it is worth making a short detour past the fishermen's huts to the south end of the quay. Erosion of the lower cliff section in the south-east corner (SY908787) has produced probably the most interesting archaeological section[42] on the Dorset coast. At the base is a series of convex layers of reddish and grey shale *(36, 1)*. The red colouring shows that the shale has been burnt in a well ventilated fire.[43] The shape of the layers suggests that the burnt material accumulated into a mound. These layers have produced pieces of moulded clay likely to be the remains of salt making in the Iron Age – Romano-British period – a topic which will be considered later. Overlying, and therefore later than these layers, is a thick deposit of mostly unburned shale of small irregularly jumbled blocks *(36, 2)*. The disordered arrangement shows that this is redeposited shale and is almost certainly related to the industrial activities of the sixteenth, seventeenth or nineteenth centuries. The latest features in the section are the wall of limestone blocks *(36, 3)* and the trench dug through the mound *(36, 4)* to accommodate it. These are heavily burnt (the dark reds are due to

36 Cliff section, Kimmeridge Bay. See text for explanation of annotation.

37 Kimmeridge Bay: a post surviving from the nineteenth-century wooden pier (1), footings of a nineteenth-century stone pier (2)

oxidised iron minerals in the limestone) and appear to be part of an industrial structure, probably of the nineteenth century.

At the time of writing the base of the section had been damaged, apparently by inquisitive digging. *Please do not dig into the section. Help to preserve this priceless piece of heritage for people to study in the future.* It is already at terminal risk from marine erosion.

Other features of the post-medieval coastal works are visible from the southern and western sea wall at mid-tide or lower. The vertical post *(37, 1)* is part of a nineteenth-century wooden pier, and the massive footings in the background *(37, 2)* are those of the nineteenth-century stone pier, which was seen from Hen Cliff. If the tide is low enough, some of the stonework associated with the seventeenth-century pier and dock can be traced to the north *(38)*.

Back on the coast path, near where it passes the toilets in the higher boat park, there is a view of the north slope of Hen Cliff below Clavel Tower. The terracing does not appear quite like the contour strip lynchets seen elsewhere. There do appear to be some on this slope, but the most prominent disturbance is the track of the nineteenth-century tramway mentioned earlier, which linked inland shale mines with processing and shipping sites near the shore.

38 A seventeenth-century pier and dock, Kimmeridge Bay

Crossing the stream gives a better view of the dragon's teeth and pillbox. The surface of the latter shows the furrows left by the corrugated iron sheeting used as shuttering when the concrete was poured. Pillboxes were almost always made of reinforced concrete (as in the case of the first example seen at Studland), but when wood was not available for shuttering other means were used. Another common solution was to use brickwork as shuttering, and then leave it *in situ* (as seen on the Cuddle).

So far, three different ground plans of concrete pillbox have been encountered: irregular hexagon at Studland, square at the Cuddle, and cylindrical here (plus the steel Alan Williams Turret at Seacombe). This seems a good point to introduce pillbox typology, which can then be used as shorthand for classification of the many others that will be seen. The forms[44] which cover most of those on the Dorset coast are:

hexagonal	Type 22 (regular)
hexagonal	Type 24 (5 sides equal and one longer side)
cylindrical	Type 25
square	Type 26

There are also variants on these: the one examined at Studland, for example, was not quite a Type 24.

Note: The text now assumes access to the coast path on military land between this point and Lulworth. Beware that this access is only available on most (not all) weekends and during public holidays.

The guide may refer to locations which are not on the marked Range Walks. Do not attempt to get to these locations. The MOD does not permit walkers to leave the marked paths.

Beyond the modern oil well, examples of contour and cross-contour strip fields can be seen on the hillside to the north; south of the path, at SY 898789, the top of another pillbox is visible from the scrub. Immediately to its east there is a ditch running north-south to the cliff, which does not appear to be related to the natural drainage. It also appears that material from the ditch has been piled in a bank to its west, possibly against the pillbox at its southern end. Inaccessibility prevents more thorough assessment of this feature.

From here, looking north-west towards the Portland beds of Gad Cliff, the coast path can be seen crossing a prominent mound *(39, 1)*,

39 A prehistoric salt-making site (1), Hobarrow Bay

40 Briquetage brought to the surface by animal burrowing at a prehistoric salt-making site, Hobarrow Bay

terminating just east of the path and truncated on the west side by the cliffs of Hobarrow Bay (SY892794). Close inspection may show that animal disturbance has brought to the surface reddish shale and fragments of coarse pottery of a similar colour, such as those shown in *Figure 40*. As mentioned earlier, the pink colouring indicates that the shale and the clay has been heated in an oxygen-rich fire. The fragments of coarse pottery, known as 'briquetage', are a good indication that salt boiling was the reason for the heating. Their form suggests an Iron Age or Romano-British date. When reconstructed they form shallow pans and rough bars; the latter are probably fire bars used to support the pans over a fire. It is thought that brine − seawater already concentrated by evaporation − was heated in the pans until dried into salt cakes. Containers of a similar material but of a different shape have been found on quite distant inland sites, suggesting that salt could also be transported in them, presumably in the context of trade or exchange. Salt boiling sites are almost always situated on low-lying cliffs, giving easy access to the shore, but more importantly were selected so that the shore itself provided good conditions for the initial concentration of seawater: natural evaporation. Flat areas, which

41 A ledge at Hobarrow Bay

flooded at high water and dried at low tide were needed, where the sun could evaporate seawater trapped in salt pans. The ledges of Broad Bench provided just these conditions *(41)*, and help to explain why there are at least three more salt boiling sites of this type and date in the vicinity. Hut sites probably related to the Hobarrow mound have been found to the east.[45]

To the south-east of the site, the cliff section can be seen from the path. The layer of limestone slabs about 2m below the surface are unlikely to be natural, as they bear no relation to the geological stratigraphy, and they also do not appear to relate to any medieval or later field boundaries. This suggests that they may be connected with the salt boiling site.

From here the coast path climbs to the north, first gently over the upper parts of the Kimmeridgian and then steeply crossing the Portlandian scarp. At Tyneham Cap it turns west along Gad Cliff and a view over the Wealden beds of Tyneham valley to the Chalk ridge beyond opens to the north.

View Point: Gad Cliff

Due north lies the village of Tyneham *(42, 1)*. In the conventions of field archaeology this is a deserted settlement, but it is unusual in that the reasons for its desertion are well understood: the village and nearby hamlets were evacuated in 1943 to make way for a military training area, and it has been retained in that role to the present day. For those wishing to explore the matter further there are useful interpretations in the village. This site is another illustration of the dilemmas of conservation. It is easy to spot the results of using the area as part of a firing range (trackways for military vehicles, and moving targets; the scars of shell holes, now healing; and the buildings themselves, many of which were damaged by bombardment) and to conclude that military use has been detrimental. On the other hand it could be argued that the military presence has conserved a mid-twentieth-century landscape which might have been lost to development which has changed the character of villages elsewhere and, to intensive agriculture which has eliminated so many relict farming landscapes. This is not the place to consider value judgements on these points of view, but to notice that conservation problems rarely have simple or completely satisfactory solutions.

This is a good vantage point from which to think about land boundaries. Boundaries are important to the landscape archaeologist: for what purpose; when and by whom has the land been divided up to create the pattern seen today? The definition of space is a deeply significant psychological and social phenomenon controlling the way people behave – think about the implications of 'sitting room' or 'beach hut' or

42 Tyneham village (1), one of its medieval open fields (2), Baltington (3), the estate boundary between Baltington and Tyneham, which is of Saxon date (4), Tyneham valley

'church'. Probably every page in this book has an implicit reference to defined spaces of one kind or another. Spatial boundaries of all scales can be seen from this viewpoint: rooms within houses (cupboards within rooms if Tyneham were still occupied) and houses within gardens. These are physical boundaries, but houses and gardens lie within a village whose boundary is less definite, more conceptual. Outside the village there are somewhat different nested boundaries: farmhouses within farmyards within systems of fields, and there are boundaries between farms at the limits of these systems. The lynchets of celtic fields have been seen at Kingston Down and medieval strip lynchets at several places. These must have had defined boundaries before the lynchets were formed by repeated ploughing. How substantial these were is often unknown, and excavation elsewhere shows a wide range of possibility: fences, hedges, walls, banks and ditches have all been found. Local materials, function, date and social context all play a part in determining any particular case. The smaller fields bounded by hedges in the Tyneham valley contrast with the much larger enclosed areas on the ridges to north and south. Part of the reason for this is functional: the arable land was in the valley and required a tighter measure of control of stock than the areas on the higher ground and steeper slopes which tended to remain pasture. But equally, or more important, are social reasons. Around medieval settlements, particularly in the east of Dorset, there were two or three large fields, each with a physical boundary, but within each were groups of strips probably held and worked individually within a communally agreed agricultural pattern. One of these open fields can be seen north of the church *(42, 2)*. Beyond these was communal grazing. By the post-medieval period, this peasant-based system of farming had been replaced by one in which sheep had become dominant, agricultural practice was improving and landholding was concentrated in the hands of fewer, richer, people. These changes led to the enclosure of the open fields to produce the surviving pattern of small, somewhat irregular, fields near the settlements. The common grazing was also enclosed, but rather later, producing the much more regular pattern of large fields.

There are also larger scale boundaries of much interest here. Christopher Taylor used this area (among others near the coastal strip which are less easy to appreciate) to illustrate the longevity of some land boundaries.[46] He argued that there were four estates in existence in the late eleventh century. Three of them are represented by the remains of farms at Baltington *(42, 3)*, North Egliston *(colour plate 9, right-hand side)* and South Egliston, and the fourth by Tyeham village itself. Each of these settlements (earthworks at Baltington and South Egliston suggest they were once larger than single farms) lie at the centre of a block of land defined by boundaries which run continuously north–south across the valley, from ridge top to ridge top. The boundary separating Baltington and Tyneham is indicated in *Figure 42, 4*; that separating Tyneham and North Egliston cuts diagonally across colour plate 9 from the bottom left corner. These boundaries, which date from at least the Saxon period, are still functional (though in a slightly different role) and are as prominent as any in the landscape. Elsewhere, some large-scale land boundaries have been shown to have even earlier origins, and it is possible that these are pre-Saxon, as there is abundant evidence of Romano-British and Iron Age settlement in the immediate vicinity. For example, the Iron Age hillfort, Flowers Barrow, dominates the western end of the Chalk ridge *(colour plate 10)*.

FROM GAD CLIFF TO LULWORTH

Considering first the Romano-British evidence: As the path heads westwards towards Worbarrow Tout it descends Gold Down to pass Pondfield Cove (SY871796), still defended by Second World War anti-tank blocks. Here and at the foot of the Tout are outcrops of the Upper Purbeck Beds, including Purbeck marble; the location is a diminutive mirror image of the exposure at Peveril Point. At that location the exploitation of Purbeck marble in the Romano-British period was discussed and the possibility that the outcrop at Peveril attracted the attention of 'Roman' prospectors. It is also possible that the outcrop here was noticed, and the existence of a settlement of that period at SY869800[47] *(10)* may be relevant in this context. Most of the site has probably been destroyed by cliff erosion, but from excavation and cliff collection it appears to have been occupied through the Iron Age and Romano-British periods. Among the finds were a Purbeck marble loom weight, and a fragment of a part-finished mortarium[48]. The latter were made in pottery and stone, and the stone ones were usually made from Purbeck marble at this time. This example was of another Purbeck

43 Flowers Barrow Iron Age hillfort from the north

limestone, the finished appearance of which is not greatly dissimilar to Purbeck marble. It is possible that this site was involved in the manufacture of objects from these rocks; the manufacturing site at Norden near Corfe Castle might be a larger-scale analogy.[49]

Before crossing the stream, note an Allen-Williams turret (with an interpretation panel) east of the remains of the fisherman's cottage, near the modern flagpole. In the steep ascent to Rings Hill, the path passes a Type 25 pillbox on the cliff-edge, crosses deeply defined celtic field boundaries, and reaches the crest in the earthworks of the Iron Age site, with which the fields are probably associated. It is the most visually impressive archaeological site on the Dorset coast: Flowers Barrow Hillfort,[50] though its general appearance is best appreciated from the road near Lulworth Castle *(43)*.

It will be tempting here to explore the hillfort, but please heed the MOD signs and do not stray from the marked paths.

The coast path passes a Second World War observation post and enters the south-east corner of the hillfort, where the gaps in the ramparts and ditches mark an original gateway *(44)*. In the outer rampart, further to the north, there is another gap *(44, 1)* but in this case, the outline of the ditch continues unbroken in front of it (though it has been partially filled) showing that this gap is not original. Across the ridge, beyond the enclosure to the east, there is another length of bank and ditch[51] which may be an additional earthwork strengthening the defence of this easy approach. In the Iron Age the site almost certainly had a complete circuit of high banks and deep ditches, but on the south side these have been eroded by the encroaching cliff *(45)*. The site probably began as an enclosure with a single bank and ditch in the early Iron Age, with a second bank and ditch being added, probably in the late Iron Age, to give the arrangement seen today. Under favourable lighting conditions and winter vegetation, traces of circular depressions can be seen in the interior, which are probably the sites of houses. The depression around the inside of the inner rampart is the remains of a quarry for material to supplement the bank. The interior almost certainly contains storage pits; one was excavated in 1939[52] – the only excavation to have taken place on this site. There have been excavations at many hillforts, and from these we might infer that, when occupied in the late Iron Age, the ramparts at Flowers Barrow were probably clean white chalk steeply

44 The eastern entrance from the inner rampart: later gap in outer rampart (1), Flowers Barrow

45 The interior of Flowers Barrow hillfort from the west

46 The view west from the western end of Flowers Barrow: Bindon Hill Iron Age rampart (1), earthwork of uncertain date (2)

sloping into 'V-shaped' ditches. Earlier, the ramparts may have been breasted or strengthened with timber-work (see Bindon Hill, below), and there would have been a strong wooden gate.

How is this site to be understood, and related to contemporary sites in the area? Hillforts are rare compared to simpler occupation sites; three hillforts will be seen on the path, and perhaps there are ten times that number of other Iron Age occupation and industrial sites nearby. Hillforts are almost always in prominent positions and they give every impression of being defended: they have massive banks and ditches with steep sides and sometimes parapets, elaborate gateways (at Flowers Barrow, for example, a vulnerable approach has an additional defensive structure); earthworks become more elaborate with time, and many hillforts have pits containing hoards of pebbles thought to be sling stones. So they could have been functionally defensive. But they could also, or alternatively, be demonstrations of power and status – a bit like the all-terrain vehicle today, which symbolises the power to consume and the power to drive anywhere, but is only used in the conquest of the occasional kerb. There is also the question of occupation. Some hillforts were quite densely and continuously occupied, and show a high level of internal organisation, while in others occupation seems rather slight. So it is not possible to conclude that hillforts were defended towns, or that they were enclosures where people sought shelter in times of danger. They may have been both, but it does seem likely that they were at least locations of power and, controlled by those who held power over local groups. The larger tribal affiliations of these hillfort builders is known in the sense that they share material culture thought to represent the Durotriges, but the nature of the sub-tribal groups which might be reflected in the distribution of hillforts is quite unknown.

From the western end of the hillfort, there is a good view of Bindon Hill to the west, on which there is an enclosure which is of much interest, and is to be discussed below. Its rampart *(46, 1)* can be traced westwards from above the clump of trees, Bindon Plantation.

Leaving the hillfort across the western ramparts, the coast path descends to Arish Mell and passes the foot of a small hill which has largely been eroded by the sea. Looking down on this hill under favourable lighting there appears to be a hollow, encircling what remains of its northern shoulder, terminated by the cliff at east and west *(46, 2)*.

Little attention has been paid to this feature in the literature, but it seems sufficiently coherent to suggest that it may be a deliberate ditch,[53] rather than an accidental artefact produced by the bombardment the hill has suffered as an artillery target area. If that suggestion is allowed, some further attention should be given to its form: the ditch could be seen as discontinuous. Interrupted ditch construction is well known in Neolithic sites, particularly those known as Causewayed Enclosures.[54] It would be going too far to suggest that this might be a Causewayed Enclosure, but it probably merits further investigation before it is finally claimed by the sea.

Just beyond the western end of Bindon Plantation, the path crosses the eastern rampart of the enclosure on Bindon Hill.[55] This site was conceived on a remarkable scale. Looking west, its northern rampart disappears over the ridge; it can be seen to the right of the path for almost 2 ½km before it turns south around the shoulder of the hill above Lulworth. There is evidence for its construction in the early Iron Age, but it has no southern rampart, which it might be expected to have if it were a conventional hillfort. Earthworks at the western end (see below) suggest that its southern boundary may have been the sea. If this is the case, it encloses not only the whole of Bindon Hill, but also the plateau to its south from Mupe Bay to Lulworth Cove, some 160ha, making it one of the largest enclosures of its kind. Not satisfactorily classed as hillforts, sites of this type have been termed 'hill-top enclosures'.

Notice two 'star posts'[56] east of the Royal Armoured Corps memorial, which mark two Bronze Age barrows. The hollows in their tops suggest that they have been mutilated by antiquarian diggers rather than gunfire. Notice also, the series of banks and ditches, about 150m apart and each cut by the track, which cross the hill between this point and the Range Safety radar station, and particularly, note the presence of a ditch on both sides and, their sharp profiles and the sparseness of vegetation on them. These will need to be distinguished from other cross-ridge features further along the hill, and will be returned to below.

Just before reaching the Range Safety radar station, a 'star post' indicates the position of an original entrance to the enclosure, which is in the form of a 'corridor' created by turning the ramparts inwards on either side of the entrance gap *(47)*. Beyond the Range boundary

47 The Bindon Hill entrance

there is a substantial bank and ditch running north–south across the hill. This appears to cut off the western end of the enclosure as its ditch is to the east. This cross-ridge dyke has been shown by excavation to be of Iron Age date. It has some interesting details, among which is the small bank on the berm (platform) between the ditch and bank. This has been interpreted as a marking out bank, and continues beyond the south end of the earthwork, where it appears to be unfinished.

Compare this earthwork with those crossed on the ridge top. In addition to the difference in profile, notice that it shares the 'softened' appearance and turf cover of the other Iron Age earthworks: more than 2,000 years of weathering and soil forming processes has created this effect. The freshness of the other banks show that natural processes have not acted on them for such a long period, and suggests a much more recent date. Their spacing and confinement to the flat top of the ridge suggests that they may be anti-glider obstacles constructed as part of the Second World War anti-invasion defences.

48 The junction between the rampart and cross-ridge dyke, Bindon Hill

If the large Iron Age cross-ridge dyke is followed northwards, the junction between it and the main rampart can be examined *(48)*. Generally, the main rampart is rather slight, and its irregularity suggests that it is unfinished for much of its length. Avoid the temptation to trace the main rampart around the western end of the hill as furze and bramble become increasingly discouraging. The rampart can be picked up again on the west-facing slope by continuing down the spine of the hill, at a point where it terminates at another length of ditch which descends the very steep slope towards West Lulworth village *(colour plate 11)*. Another earthwork aligned with this appears south-west of the village and extends to the cliff-edge. Presumably, an interconnecting length is hidden beneath the village: its continuity is suggested by a reference in a thirteenth-century charter. The intention of the builders to enclose the plateau south of Bindon Hill seems to be indicated by the presence of these western earthworks.

It was Sir Mortimer Wheeler who undertook the small limited excavations of the ramparts at Bindon Hill in 1950 which provided the evidence for the early Iron Age date.[57] He thought that Bindon Hill was the location of a beach-head to support invaders from the continent, an idea which has not stood the test of time and changing fashion in explanations of the past. (Currently prehistorians prefer to think of Bindon Hill in rather vaguer terms of territorial definition.) The information Wheeler gathered on the likely construction of the rampart led him to undertake a small reconstruction on the site to estimate the time it might have taken to build, an action which, in his characteristically dashing style, he described as a *jeu d'esprit*, not without interest in the history of the now serious field 'experimental' or simulation archaeology.

LULWORTH TO WEYMOUTH

On the summit of Hambury Tout the path passes two well preserved Bronze Age barrows. The eastern one has a circular ditch, the inner slope of which is continuous with the slope of the hemispherical mound. This form is classified as a 'bowl barrow'. The barrow to its west, near to the triangulation point, has a different form *(49)*. Its ditch is separated from the mound by a berm; this form is classified as a 'bell barrow'. Both of these barrows appear to have been opened by an antiquary, J. Milner, in the late eighteenth century. In the bell barrow, he reported finding a crouched skeleton with a pottery vessel on its breast near the centre, and

49 Bronze Age bell barrow, Hambury Tout

beneath it, at the centre, a large heap of ashes.[58] Later there will be an opportunity to compare this early example of barrow digging with more recent excavations. There is another bowl barrow of rather flattened appearance which is on the lower ridge to the north-west.

From Hambury Tout there is a good view of the Iron Age earthworks on the western end of Bindon Hill and Lulworth Cove *(11)*.

Between Hambury Tout and White Nothe the direct route of the coast path keeps to the cliff-edge, and negotiates four deep coombes: Scratchy Bottom, Vicarage Bottom, Middle Bottom and West Bottom. An alternative path a little inland along the heads of the coombes is less arduous, and probably gives a better impression of the surface archaeology, which mainly consists of traces of prehistoric farming on the valley sides and ridges between. This is the largest group of well preserved celtic fields on the path, and field boundaries can been seen on most surfaces, but because of the varying orientations and inclinations of the topography only some will be easily seen at any time. The best time for most is probably early morning or evening, in low winter sunshine. Two thorough surveys of these earthworks[59] have not found any definite evidence of contemporary settlement, but have drawn attention to structural features in the field patterns, which suggest deliberate planning in layout and possibly definitions of prehistoric landholding or agricultural function. The round barrows within the area of the fields appear to be integrated with them. Barrows tend to be on or near field boundaries, but there appears to be no clear instance of one overlying the other. This could be because they are roughly contemporary, both early Bronze Age, or the fields could be somewhat later than the barrows. It has been suggested that in some instances barrows may have been used to lay out some of these field boundaries.[60]

A roughly square banked enclosure, the Round Pound, can be seen at SY796816, looking north from the path above Vicarage Bottom. This may be prehistoric. A piece of early Iron Age pottery has come from its bank, but this only makes a date earlier than the early Iron Age very improbable; it could be later.

The coast path passes in front of what were once coastguard cottages on White Nothe, but exploring the promontory to the south is rewarding. Most archaeologists have tended to assume that the deep 'ditch' which appears to 'defend' the promontory is a geological feature. Recently, faced with the need to say something about it in this book, I checked to see how geologists explained it, only to find they had tended to assume that it was archaeological![61] The field evidence seems to suggest a natural origin, associated with fissuring, slumping and solution processes which have occurred to its east and west. An alternative inter-pretation which attempted to suggest human agency on grounds of regularity would remain incredible in the absence of any convincing associated banks, or apparently of anything of significance to defend which could be dated to a time when an earthwork of this scale might have been constructed. However, there are two archaeological features crossing it from north to south: a causeway, and towards its western end, the boundary separating the parishes of Chaldon Herring and Owermoigne. The causeway probably dates to the early nineteenth century (see below), and the boundary is manorial, and therefore is at least early medieval.[62] The fissure, clearly, predates these. On the south side of the fissure, east and west of the causeway, there are two features which might just possibly be interpreted as dumps for intended banks. If this is what they are, the possibility that they might be indications of an abandoned attempt to fortify the fissure cannot be ruled out. It is not necessary to look far for the 'dump' technique, or for an unfinished attempt at fortification: both can be seen in the Iron Age cross-ridge dyke at Bindon Hill.

The masonry structure south of the fissure *(50)* appears to be of three (or possibly two) phases:

(1a) A fragment of curving lime mortared flint wall, and footings beneath the turf

(1b) A fragment of cement-mortared limestone rubble wall
       It is likely that these are remains of the coastguard lookout which was built along with the cottages in the later nineteenth century, and which disappears from documentary records by 1922[63]

(2)   A pillbox (Type 26) in buff brick (not brick-shuttered reinforced concrete) incorporating (1b) in its north wall

(3)   An observation post (Royal Observer Corps?) in red brick, built on top of (2)

Iron steps on the east exterior wall of (2) ascend to (3). The pillbox and the observation post may be contemporary, the pillbox having been intended as additional protection for crew of the observation post.

50 The remains of White Nothe coastguard lookout with Second World War additions

51 The Second World War radar transmitter building, Ringstead

West of this structure, the parish boundary survives as a prominent bank derived from a deep ditch on either side. To the north, beside the coast-guard cottages and beyond, it is a much slighter affair. The difference is presumably due to the absence of agricultural disturbance on the promontory, which has damaged the earthwork inland. There may be Second World War disturbance to the southern end of its eastern ditch, where it may have been deepened to form a rudimentary slit trench. There is also a circular depression on the cliff-edge to its south-west, which is probably a light weapon pit.

To the south-east of the Second World War structure, there is a slightly embanked enclosure about 10m square. This is probably associated with the Napoleonic Signalling station, which was part of the series discussed earlier at Round Down and Ballard Down.

Descending westwards from White Nothe, the path leaves the Chalk for the less resistant, and less stable, Kimmeridgian beds of Ringstead Bay. The wide sweep of the Chalk ridge forms the sky line to the north, and bears traces of strip lynchets indicating marginal cultivation in medieval times. Here the strips are slighter than those seen at Winspit; presumably because the duration of cultivation was less.

At SY758817, just east of the start of the path signed 'NT South Down ¾' on the coast path marker, there is an earth covered bunker of Second World War origin *(51)*. Its interpretation will be considered later.[64]

West of the beach shop, the gravel path passes seaward of the cottages. Looking north-west and up the hill, the angular brick and concrete structure, which can be seen beside a group of conifers, is Upton Fort, which the path passes in a kilometre or so. It now enters a short strip of woodland and emerges with a pasture on the north and reed beds to the left. Examine the field. Towards the back some roughly rectilinear earthworks will be seen *(52)*. Their regularity suggests human agency. Distinguish these from the irregular hummocks characterising the natural landscape for the next few miles, which result from local insta-bility and down-slope movement in the underlying rocks of which clay forms a large part.

The site is not open to the public but a plan of the earthworks[65] shows these to be closes and house platforms beside a hollow way (sunken track) leading south into traces of open fields in the foreground (which may be seen under low-angle lighting). The arrangement is typical of a

52 The site of a deserted medieval village, Ringstead

small deserted settlement, which is identified with West Ringstead. It is not known exactly why this settlement came to be abandoned, but it is likely to have occurred in the thirteenth or fourteenth century, when factors which include decreasing population (in some but not all cases linked to ravages of the plague), changes in land holding and agricultural practice, including the expansion of sheep farming, and possibly physical factors such as climate and soil exhaustion, led to considerable shrinkage and desertion of settlements in some parts of the country. The nearest analogous deserted settlement which has been excavated is at Holworth, about 3km to the north-east.[66] The excavation provided some information on the layout and construction of a typical house site and associated plot, and dating evidence which suggested occupation beginning at least as early as the twelfth century and ending by the fifteenth century.

For those interested in twentieth-century archaeology, it is worth taking a short detour from the coast path beyond this site. Continue along the coast path as it descends into a wooded valley, ignore the first turning to the right, and climb the other side of the valley. Follow the path beside the meadow, and then turn north into another strip of woodland along the path signed 'Spring Bottom'. Almost immediately to the right, shrouded in ivy, there is a massive concrete block, which at first sight looks like an anti-tank dragon's tooth. The location, near the top of a cliff (albeit a low cliff) and the absence of others in a linear arrangement, make this unlikely. Slightly beyond, and to the left of the path there is another, much smaller concrete block, with fixing bolts in the top, too small to be part of a defence against tanks. It is not possible to make much more of these objects without further information, but knowing that this was the site of a Second World War radar station, it is reasonable to identify the larger as one surviving member of a quartet of concrete bases, supporting, probably, a transmitter mast, and the smaller as an element of the aerial rigging.[67]

Further along the path, at SY744816, there is a massive ivy-covered mound in the trees. If approached from the north, east or west, this might at first sight appear to be a short and rather high Neolithic long barrow. But from the south, a brick and concrete entrance (now sealed) can be seen, which strongly suggests twentieth-century military architecture. This is one of the radar operational buildings, covered with a blast-proofing earth mound. Traces of the macadam which must have metalled the path to the bunker survive, as do some of the brick steps from the path to the entrance.

A second bunker, which lies in private garden, and at the time of writing has been recently cleared of trees, can be seen by taking the path east from Spring Bottom and following it to the road at SY748817 *(53)*. There is an unprotected building of Second World War appearance about 200m to its north-west and, half way up the hill to the north, among traces of medieval farming, is a hexagonal brick pillbox with a turf camouflaged roof.

The bunker seen earlier on the east side of the valley *(51)* is also part of this radar station. Its internal layout corresponds with a West Coast Chain Home 'C' Type transmitter block,[68] and 'disused masts' (now demolished) were mapped[69] 500m due west of the site.

Before the war, the Air Ministry experimental establishment, which eventually moved to Worth Matravers,[70] had developed and deployed a series of radar stations on the east and south-east coast, called Chain Home, which was capable of detecting aircraft approaching across the

53 The Second World War radar building, Ringstead

North Sea and the eastern Channel. With the occupation of France, enemy aircraft could approach Britain from the south and west and the Western Chain of radar stations was established to meet this threat. In many cases, radars were also installed to detect low-flying aircraft and, in some locations, to monitor shipping movements. The Ringstead station, constructed in 1941, was part of the Western Chain and contained high and low level systems.[71] The site was also developed as part of the Cold War Rotor early warning system.[72]

To return to the coast path from this excursion, retrace the path towards Spring Bottom and turn south at the first coast path signpost. Just after the turning there is a view of the deserted settlement over a gate from the north-west. In the wood to the right of the gate there is a fourth radar bunker, but this is shrouded in vegetation and hard to see.

The path at this point, although damaged and overgrown, has a well metalled surface and concrete kerbs. It terminates at the entrance to a featureless meadow. Does this appear to be of Second World War date? The only clue that it is associated with a later activity is the high quality of the materials and finish; this evidence alone does not permit any further inference. During the 1960s and '70s this road led into a sophisticated communications centre operated by the US Air Force. No trace remains of the huge aerials once in this field, which were part of a 'tropospheric scatter' long-range communications system.[73]

Just after the path back to the coast enters the wood, there is a surviving component of another radar aerial concrete base. Nearby, to its south is a collapsed structure of mortared limestone and some brick. This is much overgrown and cannot be identified with any certainty from what can be seen.

Having rejoined the coast path and reached the 'Spring Bottom' sign, the path westwards emerges into open country, and immediately to the north is a brick building with a concrete roof *(colour plate 12)*. It is clearly military in style, but not massive enough to be a defensive structure, and its open front identifies it as an observation post. It is apparent that it was intended to observe the approaches to Portland Harbour, and the earthworks visible 250m to the north-west locate the parent site. This is Fort Upton, a coastal defence gun battery, built at the beginning of the twentieth century and re-equipped for a similar purpose in the Second World War.[74] The top of a subterranean defensive position can be seen about 30m to the north-west of the observation post. There is a second observation post not far from the path at about SY739815. Very little can be seen of the fort itself from the coast path, the best view being from the south-west where the earthwork is lower. From here the inner ashlar revetment of the bank and some ancillary buildings can be seen *(colour plate 13)*. Avoid the temptation to take the path west from Spring Bottom to get a better view from the north. Little more can be seen from there, and some emphatic notices suggest the residents (the site is privately owned) do not welcome the curious.

As the path descends towards Osmington Mills, notice abandoned medieval strip lynchets on the slope to the north-west of the village.

At Osmington Mills the coast path walker is presented with a choice of routes, one remaining near the cliff, passing through Weymouth, around Portland and along the north shore of the Fleet to Abbotsbury. The other makes inland and onto the South Dorset Ridgeway which it follows west to rejoin the coastal route at Abbotsbury. For anyone with a particular interest in prehistory, the inland route offers the richer experience. Bronze Age barrows are always nearby (the path passes important groups on Bincombe Hill and Bronkham Hill, containing examples of most of the main forms), and permits short detours to the Neolithic bank barrow on Came Down, Chalbury Iron Age hillfort, the superb celtic field group in the Valley of Stones, the Grey Mare and Her Colts Neolithic stone chambered tomb and the Kingston Russell stone circle. However, the coastal route provides a greater variety of archaeological evidence, and the tranquil atmosphere of the Fleet on a kind day more than makes up for a few stretches of this part of the path that are archaeologically somewhat barren, so the temptation to take the inland route will be resisted in this guide.

Continuing west, the path skirts the north of the strip fields seen from the east of the village and then crosses their headlands on the crest of the ridge on Black Head. Here, as at Kimmeridge, the strips run at right angles to the contour, adding to the difficulties of ploughing. Running between the strips towards the village is a broad hollow. This is almost certainly the remains of a droveway which gave access for animals to be driven through the arable to grazing beyond. Notice how the later enclosure hedges follow orientation of the strip fields.

At first glance, the knoll on the summit of Black Head (SY723830) seems to have a ditch running around it, but closer inspection shows that it is irregular and apparently coincident with a band of harder limestone which can be seen in the cliff-edge. The 'ditch' is a series of small stone quarries.

West from Black Head the view is dominated by a landscape whose hummocky appearance reflects the unstable mixture of soft water-logging clays and limestone beneath the surface *(54)*. This is an unstable substrate and the cliff forms are dominated by rotational slumping. This would have been a hostile environment for settlement in earlier times, and is archaeologically relatively empty; only the 'holiday camp' seems to have found a recent footing. However, there are a few points of archaeological interest before the path loses itself in the urban landscape of Weymouth.

The first is on the descent from Black Head. Here the path crosses the foot of a slope on which there are well developed strip fields with terracettes on the risers *(55)*. This is a good opportunity to compare the results of what are rather similar physical processes operating at different scales under different causes. The underlying process is soil movement

54 The landscape west of Black Head, Osmington

55 Strip lynchets and terracettes, Black Head, Osmington

occurring at a non-uniform rate down the slope. In the case of the lynchets soil is destabilised by the plough and can move easily from the up-slope edge of the strip, but is slowed and stabilised by the unploughed boundary at the lower edge. Terracettes also involve destabilisation and stabilisation of soil at the upper and lower boundaries of the 'micro-lynchets', but the agent is probably mainly the habitual trampling of sheep and cattle moving and grazing around the contours of the hill.

In the vicinity of the stone coast path marker inscribed 'Weymouth 3¾' the terraces, which are almost on the same scale as strip lynchets, are much more irregular, sheer-sided and discontinuous and they are 'fresher', not much healed by nature. These do not result from human activity, but from rotational slumping of the unstable land to the south. They can be readily compared with traces of real strip lynchets on the gentle south-facing slope to the north-west.

Looking west towards Weymouth from the south-west corner of the holiday camp activity centre, note the cylindrical concrete Second World War Type 25 pillbox at about SY717817. Its position on the beach results from cliff erosion since the war.

From the first crest of Redcliff Point, SY712816, a view of the chalk downland of the South Dorset Ridgeway opens up to the north. In the area of the Ridgeway enclosing the river Frome around and west of Dorchester, the density of prehistoric sites, particularly of the second and third millennia BC, equals those of Cranborne Chase and the areas of Salisbury Plain around Stone Henge and Avebury. As in those areas, there are high concentrations of long barrows and later round barrows, and these seem to be clustering around centres of ritual activity, huge round enclosures of earth, timber and stone – Causewayed Enclosures and henge monuments, and the mysterious long enclosures – cursus monuments. Unfortunately, only round barrows from this ritual landscape can be seen from here, but at least a dozen should be visible on the distant ridge *(56)*.

An Iron Age hillfort, Chalbury, is also visible from here *(56, 1)*. Chalbury has been more fully explored by excavation than most of the other hillforts encountered on the Heritage Coast, though even here work was limited to an examination of the defences and a small area of the interior.[75] These excavations suggest fortification and occupation of the hilltop in the early Iron Age. The site has a simple rampart of earth

56 South Dorset Ridgeway from Redcliff Point: Chalbury Iron Age Hillfort (1)

and stone dug from a ditch and internal quarries with an entrance to the south-east. The slight hollows representing round houses and storage pits can still be seen on the surface.

Medieval strip lynchets can be seen stranded on the slopes of the Ridgeway above the settlements of Sutton Poyntz and Bincombe.

Immediately beside the path at this point are two hollows a couple of metres in diameter, and of fairly crisp appearance (*56*, foreground). The latter suggests they are not of great age, and closer inspection shows that one of them contains rusting iron sheet. These are typical of Second World War 'dugouts' quite commonly inserted at good vantage points such as these; there are several examples in the ramparts of hillforts. Sometimes pieces of angle iron also protrude from them. They are usually explained in terms of military exercises or the activities of the Home Guard.

From the western crest of Redcliff Point, the view to the north-east now includes the nineteenth-century chalk-cut representation of George III, which recognises his patronage of the seaside resort of Weymouth.

57 Jordan Hill Romano-British temple

The prominent 1.5m-high lynchet, which the path follows west from Redcliff Point, marks the location of a former field boundary. Ploughing has produced the smoother surface to the north which is lower due to soil movement down the slope. Looking up the path from the 'Weymouth 2¼' coast path marker, the footings of a dry stone wall can be seen coinciding with the boundary. In the hedge beside the gate, the standing stone marks the boundary between the parishes of Osmington and Weymouth.

Before picking up the coast path again beyond Weymouth, it is worth following the sign to the Jordan Hill Romano-British Temple, SY698811, north of the road from Bowlease Cove to Weymouth. The site was excavated in the nineteenth century and produced evidence suggesting the ritual deposition in a shaft of birds and artefacts, presumably in connection with the deity associated with the location. As some of the deposits can be linked to the symbolism of the Celts, it is likely that the temple gives expression to a local Iron Age deity in Romano-British style. There is further occupation evidence in the area, suggesting a site of some complexity.[76] It is an interesting example of a minimal reconstruction becoming an alternative kind of archaeological field evidence, and invites reflection on the impression of the past that might be conveyed by what is presented here *(57)*.

FROM WEYMOUTH HARBOUR TO FERRYBRIDGE

The coast path is best rejoined at the eastern end of the south side of the harbour, where it passes the Nothe Fort. The exterior views of this coastal defence fort show elements of nineteenth- and twentieth-century use. It is now a museum, which interprets its history.

The view to the south is across the Bincleaves Groyne of Portland Breakwater. Some of the features associated with it are archaeological, in the sense adopted here, as they are mostly no longer used. None are accessible: they were formerly in Admiralty or Government Research Establishment hands and are now in private ownership. At this distance nothing can be inferred about their purpose. The buildings on the Groyne itself were used in connection with the research and development of underwater weapons.

To avoid this complex, the path turns inland. Towards the end of its coincidence with Sandsfoot Road there are public gardens to the east and beyond these a ruinous structure, Sandsfoot Castle. *(58)* This was built as part of the Harbour defences by Henry VIII, probably in 1541.[77] Although access is rather limited, and much of the ashlar masonry cladding has gone, examination is worthwhile. Enough survives to

58 Sandsfoot Castle

illustrate the shapes of window and door mouldings and the portcullis slot can be seen on the north jamb of the outer door of the gate tower.

Shortly, the coast path leaves Sandsfoot Road and climbs onto a macadamised track. Notice how level the track is, how gently it curves, that here it is on an embankment and that in the verges there are traces of broken stone. These are all characteristics of an abandoned railway line: the stones are the ballast into which sleepers carrying the rails were set. This was the railway from Weymouth to Portland, which was opened in 1865 and closed in 1952. From here to Ferrybridge the walker follows the track and has an opportunity to sample 'railway archae-ology'.[78] At the entrance to the slight cutting, notice that the path deflects slightly to the east to coincide with a curbed concrete track. To its west in the centre of the cutting, traces of ballast (in which pieces of clinker from steam locomotives may be found) and a platform can be seen in the undergrowth *(59)*. This is what remains of Wyke Regis halt, later the point of transit for workers at the Whitehead Torpedo factory which operated to the west of the railway line between 1891 and 1966. A housing estate now occupies the site of the factory. The concrete track is worth further examination. It appears to terminate in a double width section south of the station, and probably turns north-west across the railway line north of it. It looks like Second World War concrete, and appears to have been constructed to bear considerable weight.[79] Possibly, this was the point for the transfer of freight from rail to road bound for Portland dockyard (for example, tanks for D-Day disembarkation), which was too heavy to complete its journey over the Smallmouth rail bridge. Southwards on the shore at SY668762 (note in passing, the concrete fence posts typical of railway boundaries, and note their condition for comparison with other examples later), traces of the piers of this bridge can be seen *(60)*. There are two *in situ* cast-iron pillar bases and, fragments of concrete pillars have been reused as sea defences nearby. Look at the material used as track ballast and as filler in the concrete pillars. Is there a connection to be made between them? Possibly. Track ballast may have the most convenient source of raw material for the pillars.

59 Wyke Regis railway station and the Second World War concrete roadway

60 Small Mouth railway bridge pier bases

PORTLAND

Until recently, the coast path ignored Portland and headed west along the north shore of the Fleet at Ferrybridge. It now skirts much of the peninsula and gives access to one of the archaeologically richest sections of the coast. Portland Castle (SY685744) falls outside the scope of this guide, as English Heritage provides on-site interpretation, though it should be associated conceptually with Sandsfoot Castle as its function is complementary. Beyond it in the harbour near Portland Port (the old Naval Base), there are two building-size concrete boxes which meet the criterion of abandonment appropriate for inclusion here *(61)*. The absence of windows, however, suggests that they are not conventional buildings, but the by-now familiar concrete of the 1940s suggests a wartime function. There are others like this on the Normandy coast near Arromanches, in which context they would be easier to recognise as elements of the Mulberry Harbours which provided an essential temporary port for the D-Day invasion, Operation Overlord. Sections of harbour like these were fabricated at sites around the coast of Britain before being towed across the channel; the two in Portland Harbour were never used for this purpose.

The path to Portland Heights climbs the north scarp of the Portlandian rocks that dominate the landscape to the south. From the viewpoint in the car park at SY690731, there is a spectacular view of Chesil Beach and the Fleet *(62)*. This is a good place from which to observe a terrace which slopes down from the Verne Citadel, a huge Victorian fortified barracks built by convict labour, which became, and remains, a prison. The terrace *(62, 1)* is part of the Merchants' Railway built in the 1820s to transport stone from the quarries on the high ground to the quayside. On the steepest incline, trucks were coupled in a continuous loop on parallel rails, the gravitational energy of the descending laden trucks being used to pull the empty ones back to the top.

The coast path follows the road towards the Verne, crossing the huge crevasses created by the intensive quarrying to build the Breakwater which then served as ditches of the fortification, and passes north of two other significant defensive sites. The first, some 100m south-east of the path, is a heavy anti-aircraft artillery battery, built as part of the Portland Harbour defences in the Second World War. This is one of the few

61 Portland Harbour, Mulberry Harbour components

62 Chesil Beach from Portland Heights: Merchants' Railway incline (1)

63 High Angle Battery, Portland

64 A Second World War and Cold War radar station near the Verne, Portland

remaining sites of this type in good condition in the region, but now it is used as a stable and is not accessible to the public.

Readily accessible, and provided with a useful interpretation panel near the entrance to the Verne, is the next site south of the path, the High Angle Battery *(63)*. Built in 1892 to defend the approaches to Portland Harbour, the concrete emplacements of the massive guns and protective earth banks can readily be examined: details such as the gun mounting bolts and the track of the railway serving them with ammunition can be seen. Underground elements also survive. There is an associated earthwork enclosure, the Redoubt, to the west.

East of the High Angle Battery there is a military site which appears to have been decommissioned relatively recently. Several phases of construction can be seen from outside the fence *(64)*. Six small block-like buildings, some associated with mast bases, have the appearance of an early post-Second World War radar site. Later, a single building in reconstituted stone has been added and, both clad in 'crazy-paving', a guard house and a building carrying remains of mast supports on its roof. There are also indications of entrances to underground bunkers. During the war the site had several very short wavelength ('centimetric') radars for high- and low-level surveillance,[80] and after the war the site was developed as part of the Cold War Rotor early warning system.[81]

The cliff-edge to the east of this site is also of great interest, although slightly off the path. Here there are the remains of three closely spaced observation posts (and the ruins of a fourth to the north), presumably connected with gunnery ranging. Each is a concrete structure comprising a single room with a large observation window giving a 180° view of the sea, and a small porch from which three steps ascend to ground level *(colour plate 14)*. The entrance is flanked by triangular revetments of the kind which support entrances through blast protection banks on some Second World War buildings (e.g. the bunkers at Ringstead, and the CHL station at St Aldhelm's Head) though here there are only rudimentary earthworks on the seaward side. The internal surfaces show details of the shuttering used in the construction of the walls. In addition to the more common casts of shuttering planks, there are casts of vertical and semi-horizontal framing timbers to which the planking was attached, some of which still contain traces of wood.

The coast path heads south-east, reaching the cliff-edge beside The Grove, now a Young Offenders' Institution, but originally the Victorian prison built in the mid-nineteenth century to house convicts who were employed to quarry stone required for the Portland Harbour Breakwater and the Verne Citadel. Just to the north of the secure compound, notice the two neglected buildings east of the road. These are an engine shed and workshops connected with the railway serving the Admiralty Quarries, and stand at the top of the incline on which construction began in 1848 to transport stone to the shore for the building of the Breakwater.[82]

From here there is an opportunity for some pseudo-aerial archae-ology, as the cliff top overlooks many years of activity on the narrow plateau beside the shore. Below there are the abandoned buildings of a Defence Research Establishment and, near the south end of the Breakwater, the remains of the nineteenth-century East Weares Batteries. The track of the railway, which was encountered near Ferrybridge, can be seen curving along the seaward edge of the plateau. The easiest field remains to identify comprise three prism-shaped earth mounds, the most southerly being the largest and most distinct *(65)* and in form characteristic of the butt of a rifle range. With the aid of binoc-ulars, the mechanism for raising and lowering targets can be seen behind the centre mound.

Beyond the garden of the former Prison Governor, immediately west of the path at SY704720, there are two Second World War buildings, behind an original safety rail along the cliff-edge. To the south, the larger brick building has the remains of a mast base on its roof and supporting buttresses in the walls *(66)*; there is a smaller concrete building to its north. This configuration is typical of a coastal defence radar station. The larger building was the main transmitter and receiver block, and the standby-set, for use in the event of the main equipment being put out of action, was housed in the smaller building. This is the only surviving example of a coastal defence radar station on the Dorset coast path.

Below on shore, there is a derrick for lifting stone, similar to those represented by the holes in the ledge seen at Winspit *(67)*. Nearer to Portland Bill a closer look can be taken at similar cranes. Note to the south what appears to be a pillbox camouflaged with a cladding of Portland stone.

As the path approaches Castle Cove, notice the terrace which once carried the railway up the cliff from just above sea level. The point where it plunged into a deep cutting which took it inland towards Weston can

65 A rifle range below East Cliff, Portland

66 The Second World War coastal defence radar station, The Grove, Portland

67 A derrick and a, probably camouflaged, pillbox, Durdle Pier, Portland

68 The track of the old railway entering a tunnel near Rufus Castle, Portland

69 Rufus Castle, Portland

70 St Andrew's Church, Portland

just be seen *(68, 1)*. The imposing stone structure on the cliff which comes into view as the path begins to descend towards Church Ope Cove is Rufus Castle *(69)*. It is not accessible to the public and only the north and south elevations can be seen from the path, but enough is visible to indicate its defensive nature including: its position, strong ashlar cladding, and the remains of corbelling which would have supported a parapet; the circular holes are gun ports. This is the only castle which has medieval origins on the Dorset Coast. Originally constructed in the twelfth century to protect the Royal Manor of Portland – functionally similar in this respect to Corfe Castle, though on a much smaller scale – it presumably also served as a coastal defence.[83]

Below the castle, to the south, are the remains of St Andrew's Church *(70)*. Construction of the present building began in the thirteenth century, probably on the site of an earlier church, and it was eventually demolished in 1756 after a landslip in the previous century, which had made it unsafe. The helpful interpretation board which summarises the main sequence of development should be studied before descending the steps, as there is no interpretation at the site.

This is the point on the path from which it is probably easiest to detour for a closer look at two stone towers in the centre of the island, one of which is shown in *Figure 71*. At first sight their shape may suggest that they are defensive, perhaps some kind of castle, but they

71 A windmill, Portland

72 A quarry derrick, East Cliff, Portland

lack details that would be needed to support this idea. For example, they do not possess a strong outer cladding of close-jointed ashlar masonry or battlements, and the windows, which are not notably narrow, are not positioned to give a good field of fire. If their original wooden structures were still in place they would be easily identified without specialist knowledge, as these details would include sails: the structures are windmills. It is certain that they were in use early in the seventeenth century and probable that they were built 100 years earlier. They went out of use as mills in the nineteenth century, but in the twentieth one of them appears to have been used as a Home Guard lookout,[84] so speculation about the defensive purpose of these sites would not have been completely misguided.

From Castle Cove to the Bill of Portland, the coast path runs through or beside disused cliff quarries. They are full of detailed evidence of stone extraction and there are many examples of dressed and partially dressed blocks which yield information about preparation before shipment. These details invite comparison with what has been seen between Durlston and Winspit. Lifting was done by derricks, three of which survive on the cliff-edge. Their function in this position would have been to lift stone into boats, much having been despatched by sea before land transport became a viable alternative (shown in *figure 72*). Beside the crane is a stone, on the surface of which pits have been cut *(72, 1)*.

73 A cliff-edge spoil tip, East Cliff, Portland: tramway sleeper blocks (1)

74 Strip fields (1) and Mesolithic site (2), Culver Well, Portland

These provided a location for a scissor-like clamp, a device of great antiquity which tightened in proportion to the force exerted on it by the crane to which it was attached. Some of the spoil was dumped into the sea; an example of a spoil heap extending seawards is shown in *Figure 73*. Examination of the two parallel rows of widely spaced stones on top will reveal the holes left by studs set into each one *(73, 1)*. These would have fixed the rails of a tramway on which the spoil would have been carried in small trucks. Note, in some places, the very regular cut surfaces of the working faces. These result from the use of a mechanical channelling machine to isolate blocks, later to be prised free from their bedding.[85] This technique does not appear to have been used in Purbeck.

When the path rises above the cliff quarries, the view to the north-west shows groups of medieval field strips which still influence the appearance of the farmed landscape *(74, 1)*. Below these *(74, 2)*, is the site of the earliest archaeological evidence encountered on the coast path so far. The hut is all that makes it visible, as the evidence, primarily a substantial shell midden, is either below ground or has already been removed by archaeological excavations over many years.[86] These have revealed traces of the tools and food remains of groups of people who exploited the Portland shore. At least part of their economy was based on gathering shellfish: the midden contained mostly winkles, topshells and limpets. Their tool kit included points flaked from very small pieces of stone. Among the uses to which these were put was the arming of arrows used with the bow to hunt small game. These tools are classified as Mesolithic, and they belonged to the last people in Britain to survive primarily by hunting and gathering. This was six or seven thousand years ago, when the northern hemisphere had warmed after the last Ice Age, mixed oak woodland covered much of lowland Britain, and before herding and crop growing had become established as the main form of subsistence. The material for their stone tools is interesting. Elsewhere, groups such as these would have used mainly flint as their raw material, but here at Portland people used the local equivalent form of silica (chert), an indication that they were sensitive to the properties of the inorganic resources around them. This material is quite easy to recognise, and studies of stone tools from sites of this period over the whole of south-west England show that they often contain a small proportion made from Portland chert, this proportion tending to decrease with increasing distance from Portland.[87] One way of explaining this observation is to suppose that the people who obtained their raw materials at Portland moved around, sometimes making tools elsewhere, sometimes losing tools and, perhaps, also exchanging them for other goods with other groups, thus gradually dispersing the material away from its source. The living arrangements of these Mesolithic people are not well understood, but seem normally to have been rather temporary at any one location. There is some evidence to suggest that they were adapted to a semi-migratory existence within a territory that in over a year could supply their economic needs, but required them to move from habitat to habitat as the seasonal cycle offered resources in different places; for example, at one time in woodland where nuts and fruits could be gathered, at another in upland areas where migratory game might have been taken. The generally slight traces of their encampments seem to reflect this transient activity. Some more substantial and apparently seasonally revisited sites might have been 'base camps' to which a group might regularly return. It would probably not be unreasonable to think of this site at Portland in these terms. Its relatively abundant evidence suggests more than ephemeral use, so it may have 'base camp' status, or the relia-bility of seafood resources in the region might have encouraged people to visit it frequently.

From Portland Bill the path turns north-west to climb towards the coastguard look-out. Current maps[88] show three circular masts at about SY676691. These have been dismantled, but it is worth attempting to trace their 'ghosts'. Removal of above ground structures and possibly the remains of subsoil features, which comprise the outer circles and internal patches, were distinguishable from the mature grassland in two ways at the time of writing. The features carry sparser vegetation and a different community of plants to that on undisturbed soils nearby. These will 'heal' with time if they are only the result of disturbance, but are likely to be visible for some years: they may survive for many years if sub-surface features remain.

The coast path continues north along the cliff-edge. Beyond the former Admiralty Underwater Weapons Research Establishment, a view to the north-east opens and the stone towers of the windmills mentioned earlier can be seen in the middle distance.

On the south-west corner of the modern housing estate of Weston is a mobile telephone mast. Beside it, in the corner of the estate, is a disused Royal Observer Corps post (SY681712). During the Cold War there was a network of such posts covering the whole country. Each was manned by a small crew who, in the event of a nuclear attack, would have measured blast pressures and radioactive fallout, relaying this information to a regional control bunker which would have plotted the extent of the devastation. These sites can usually be recognised by the presence of a concrete entry hatch sealed by a locked manhole cover, ventilation shaft and possibly something remaining of the instrumentation platforms.[89] A better example will be seen later near Abbotsbury.

The path now approaches Blacknor Fort (SY679716). Aesthetically, the Fort itself is somewhat disturbing, but it is a good site for attempting to work out roughly when various features were added from the materials used. It began as a coastal battery built at the beginning of the twentieth century, was re-equipped and developed for coastal and anti-aircraft defence during the Second World War and has recently been adapted to domestic use. Rendered brick and concrete are common in the original structures, brick in the Second World War, and breeze block, wood and plastic more recently. Consider too, the changes in defensive function and symbolism with time; contrast recent barbed wire and security lights with the façade of the Victorian rampart. Views of the earlier work are best from the west and north *(75)*, but at the time of writing a detour taking the path inland to avoid an unsafe section was in force, which prevented access to these prospects.

75 Blacknor Fort from the north

76 A bridge carrying the tramway to the cliff-edge spoil tip (1), a blocked tramway tunnel (2), the cliff-side tramway (3), the quarrying landscape, West Weares, Portland

South-east of the Fort, on the edge of the modern housing, is the remains of a Second World War gun emplacement, and south-west of the Fort, on a ledge cut into the cliff top, is an observation post of the same date *(colour plate 15)*. Beside this is a semi-circular concrete platform which appears to be a base for a centrally pivoted device running on a wheeled support, capable of turning through a west-facing arc of about $180°$ towards the west. Without specialist knowledge this is about the limit of deduction from the field evidence alone, but it has been said that this is the remains of a launching device for rocket testing experiments which were carried out in this vicinity[90] before the war. There is an identical base near the cliff-edge to the north of the Fort.

If the cliff path northwards remains closed, some other very interesting archaeological details will be inaccessible. Among these are the branches of quarry tramways which terminate here at the cliff-edge in waste tipping sites. There are several of these, broadly similar in concept, but differing in detail and probably in date. They can be recognised by

77 Cliff-side tramway detail, West Weares, Portland

a gully heading inland, more or less overgrown or blocked by material from later spoil. At the cliff-edge there is a modification to the rock which may include worked stones with traces of wheel ruts and metal fittings, remnants of a mechanism for braking and tipping the trucks. In several cases tramways reach the cliff at two levels, the higher being carried over another tramway running parallel with the cliff (and with which the path coincides for much of the time) by a bridge, the supporting piers of which are still standing. In one case the bridge itself is of stone *(76, 1)* and beside it there are the remains of what appears to be a blocked tramway tunnel *(76, 2)*. Nearby *(76, 3)*, the cliff-side tramway is of particular interest, as it shows distinctly the ruts left by stone carts in the underlying rock, and on a slight slope, grooves which have been made in the surface to provide grip for the horses pulling them *(77)*. All along this stretch of path there are abandoned stone blocks, many weighing many tonnes, many dressed and partly dressed: a splendid place to browse the results of stone cutting processes.

As the coast path approaches the north end of Portland it passes Tout Quarry, which is well worth exploring. There is much to see of the processes of stone quarrying dressing and transport, including some striking dry-stone tramway bridgework. One of these has the additional interest of carrying not only a dated, but a signed sequence of use. Each event is also marked by the use of a building material characteristic of its time: the original dry-stone construction in 1862, initial blocking with brick in 1944, final blocking with breeze blocks in 1972 *(78)*. The earlier nineteenth-century bridgework of Lano as effectively signifies pride in craftsmanship as it accomplishes its functional engineering purpose *(79)*.

Although this quarry is no longer worked for stone, it is by no means abandoned, having become a 'studio-gallery' for sculptural modification of surfaces left by the quarrymen. The effect may have particular resonance for those familiar with the modification of surfaces and spaces encountered in the prehistoric record and this is also a particularly exciting place to reflect on the meaning of objects. Everywhere there is a sense of ambiguity: are these sculpted blocks to be seen as embellished waste, or is the waste conveniently placed raw material for sculpture? In one example, lines of half-cylinder drill holes on fracture faces are the starting point for channels meandering over adjacent blocks. Or do the grooves meander towards something which looks like the remains of blasting holes? The sculptures of 'pseudo-domestic' objects are the most thought-provoking, ranging from fireplaces to fonts. These out-of-context 'things' claw at our sense of what an artefact can mean and, vividly emphasise the problems of 'understanding' the material world.

This is a place of steps. Underneath it all are the massive stepped quarry faces (and perhaps, the threshold of Portland itself), now much obscured by spoil. There are the stepped levels of tramways. There are Second World War concrete steps. There are artistic echoes of steps, which could be functional, but go nowhere – just like the others now go nowhere. And perhaps there are other layers of reflection. Are the sculpted steps a reference to steps which interconnected the radar station buildings, some of which still carry their rusting handrails *(80)*: a place from which electromagnetic pulses were sent and their echoes received during the Second World War?

Rubble from demolished buildings of this radar station can be seen in one of the abandoned tramways in the north east corner of the

78 A dated sequence of tramway arch construction and blocking, Tout Quarry, Portland

79 Lano's 1834 arch, Tout Quarry, Portland

80 The steps and hand rail associated with the Second World War radar station, West Cliff, Portland

81 Demolished buildings associated with the Second World War radar station, West Cliff, Portland

82 Mast bases and guy supports associated with the Second World War radar station, West Cliff, Portland

quarry *(81)*. To the south of this there are more concrete steps beside an isolated length of macadamised track leading to the top of a spoil heap where there are concrete pads *(82,* main image*)* carrying fixing eyes and other concrete emplacements from which truncated girders protrude vertically *(82,* inset*)*. Associated buildings have been demolished and pushed into an adjacent gully. Most of this, apart from the macadamised track which might be later, appears to be of Second World War origin, and the scale of the concrete bases is consistent with this having been the site of a Chain Home Low station identified with RAF Westcliff.[91]

FROM FERRYBRIDGE TO ABBOTSBURY

A feature of the coastal path along the north shore of the Fleet is the defensive line of Second World War pillboxes constructed to protect this vulnerable stretch of coast in response to the threat of German invasion. There are mostly two types in this line: the most common is hexagonal in plan, of brick and concrete (most are probably Type 22) and the

83 A Type 22 pillbox on the north shore of the Fleet near Ferrybridge

84 Strip lynchets on the north shore of the Fleet, Pirates' Cove

smaller cylindrical concrete Type 25. The first Type 22, with its protective porch breaking away, is visible from Ferrybridge (SY664764) *(83)* and there are other examples at SY660766 and SY628798; there are examples of Type 25 pillboxes at SY656769, 638791 and 624799. In most pillboxes internal features do not survive. An exception is the internal brick walling installed in some designs with the intention of limiting the damage to occupants from ricocheting projectiles and shrapnel. This can be seen in the Type 22 at SY660766.

As the path descends to the shore at Pirates' Cove, it crosses a group of well-defined strip lynchets, presumably associated with the former parish of Wyke Regis *(84)*.

Pirates' Cove may also reveal some pre-agricultural evidence. Surveys and some excavation here have recovered tools and waste products, a high proportion of which was of Portland chert.[92] The material is difficult to interpret, but can reasonably be associated with the groups of Mesolithic people, whose gathering activities accumulated at the midden at Portland, and probably represents exploitation of food resources provided by the Chesil hinterland. Small pieces of Portland chert may be seen on the surface below high water mark. Although these are not stratified, *please leave them undisturbed for others to appreciate.*

On the western limb of Pirate's Cove, an excavation in 1960[93] uncovered an area about 1m wide and 2m long delimited by limestone blocks and the cliff, which showed the characteristic colours of iron minerals which had been heated. It contained ash from the burning of Kimmeridge shale and, among the pottery which dated it to the later Iron Age there were fragments of briquetage. These features were interpreted as a salt boiling site, similar to those encountered near Kimmeridge. A source of shale for fuel was probably in the region of Ferrybridge, where there is a localised outcrop of Kimmeridge clay.

At SY652772 the path leaves the Fleet shore briefly to skirt a MOD site, at the north-east corner of which there is a pillbox. This appears to have survived an attempt at explosive demolition, as the roof has collapsed vertically and the corners have been forced apart revealing reinforcement bars not normally visible in intact structures. Where the path is displaced north again to avoid the second part of the site it is bounded on both sides by fences. On the seaward side the boundary is the current MOD fence; on the landward side it is the remains of a concrete post and wire fence. The latter appears to be the original boundary and there is a boundary marker, inscribed 'WD N° 16' set at its southern end. Similar War Department markers can be found elsewhere on the boundary of the site. The condition of the concrete fence posts is worth comparing with similar ones seen beside the track of the old railway at Ferrybridge. Posts of this kind contain iron reinforcing bars, which gradually oxidise. The oxidation products (rust) occupy a greater volume than the original bars and, as they form, exert sufficient pressure to crack and force apart the concrete, leading to spalling and disintegration. The posts here probably date to the 1940s and are in relatively good condition; those at Ferrybridge are probably at least half a century older, and they are considerably more decayed. Both have been exposed to similar environmental conditions, so the difference in their preservation may be due to the duration of their exposure. This inference requires the assumption that the quality of materials and processing were similar. Is this a reasonable assumption?

In passing through the area of landslip towards Little Sea, note the re-use of bits of military portable roadway as track metalling. Emerging east of the holiday camp, the prominent prismatic mound to its west is the butt of another firing range, inland of which the path is diverted when the range is active.

About 1½km west of the firing range the path descends to East Fleet. This is noted by most guide books for the flood of 1824, when the sea destroyed much of the village. What remained of the church was reconstructed as the chapel *(85, 1)*, and what appear to be the remains of original buildings can be seen in the undergrowth to its south *(85, 2)*. There is also a well preserved hollow way entering the settlement from the north-west between strip lynchets passing seaward of the chapel and curving north-east *(85, 3)*. 'Hollow ways' are often a feature of ancient landscapes (one was mentioned at Ringstead Deserted Medieval village, others suspected at the prehistoric settlement at Kingston Down). They are simply long-standing trackways which are eroded – hollowed – in the absence of efficient metalling, by the passage of feet, cart wheels and water.

West of East Fleet, the next two pillboxes have points of individual interest. On the roof of the first there is a block of soil, which is presumably the residue of original turf camouflage *(86)*. The second (a Type 25) has an incised graffito on its roof, which reads:

85 A chapel (1), building remains (2), a hollow way (3), East Fleet

86 A pillbox retaining some of its original turf camouflage, East Fleet

Scotland For Ever
5 [or s][?]R Callahan
Royal engineers
C.t. Has[?]
H [?]

Close examination shows that this is original, as the larger aggregate particles have been displaced by the passage of a pointed object through the wet concrete. A challenge is to decipher the rest!

To the north there are faint traces of strip fields running north-south down to the lagoon, which presumably belonged to the Manor of West Fleet. As the Moonfleet Hotel comes into view, beyond it the Iron Age hillfort of Abbotsbury Castle can be seen on the skyline and below it, St Catherine's Chapel.

The coast path turns north and makes inland away from the Fleet east of Langton Herring and the South Dorset Ridgeway reappears. From the higher ground above Wyke Wood, Hardy Monument and Bronkham Hill can be seen to the north: there are strip lynchets on its south-facing slope. The path then turns west and north again until it gains the Corallian ridge which carries it to Abbotsbury. At this point (SY596844) it crosses a wall from which well dressed steps protrude. On the west side of the wall, the path crosses another hollow way, in this case apparently a droveway which would have enabled livestock to be driven to and from permanent pasture on the ridge without interfering with the arable land surrounding Clayhanger Farm (a similar example was noted at Osmington).

Above Clayhanger Farm the Fleet once more comes into view where it widens at Abbotsbury and supports the Swannery. On the cliff-edge (at about SY579834) there is a pillbox; Second World War anti-invasion defences were strengthened around this area of the Fleet, most obviously by the double row of anti-tank blocks diagonally crossing the Chesil Beach at SY568839 *(87)*. The pits on either side of the path as it nears the end of the ridge are the remains of small limestone quarries. From this point, the strip fields below St Catherine's Chapel are strikingly lit at the end of the day. The medieval tithe barn, which would have stored part of the produce from these fields before the Dissolution of the Monasteries, is still standing in the village and is worth visiting. Looking north, the south-facing slope of the Ridgeway is covered in fields of similar age.

87 Anti-tank defences, Chesil Beach, Abbotsbury

ABBOTSBURY TO WEST BAY

At Abbotsbury the coast path again presents a choice of route: one inland following the Ridgeway, the other beside Chesil Beach. This time there is no doubt that the inland route provides the richest archaeology. On the coastal route the march of pillboxes continues along the shore; a particularly interesting example is camouflaged by its insertion in the ground floor of the lookout attached to the new coastguard cottages (SY555849); another has 'pebble-dash' camouflage. There is also a walled enclosure, once part of the eighteenth-century villa, Strangways Castle, which was badly damaged in a fire in 1913, rebuilt, then demolished in 1934 (SY556849). On the south-facing slopes near Abbotsbury medieval fields are superbly preserved. The three on Chapel Hill are divided into strips which are increasingly more etched into the slope from west to east, presumably reflecting differences in the length of time each field was under cultivation *(88)*. This guide will explore the inland route which has Bronze Age, Iron Age, medieval, post-medieval, Second World War and Cold War evidence (and although not visible, a Romano-British site).

88 Strip lynchets, south–west slope of St Catherine's Hill, Abbotsbury

89 Abbotsbury from Wears Hill, with medieval fields in foreground

Leaving the Swannery car park and climbing northwards, the path is at once in a largely medieval landscape. At first the path runs beside a mill stream, then it passes the mill, which is now a dwelling. It follows an ancient hollow way and, as it emerges from the trees, medieval agricultural traces dominate the immediate slope of Chapel Hill on the west and the more distant slopes to north and north-east, whilst to the east the tithe barn and other remains of the monastic buildings can be seen in the village.

At the main road the path turns east, passes along Back Street and turns north-west up Blind Lane, and climbs back into the Middle Ages. Blind Lane is another hollow way where it ascends the hill above the village. Further up, it becomes a 'lyncheted' track, an integral part of the open field system. Here the track retained soil to form a positive lynchet above it and defined the position of a negative lynchet below it as it was avoided by the plough.

Notice the colour of the rock where the vegetation has been worn away on the lower part of the slope: it looks like rusted iron. This is not too far from the truth, as the rock is rich in iron oxide formed from the iron released by the decomposition of ancient minerals. About halfway up the slope there is a small quarry face exposing this rock, which outcrops at several locations around Abbotsbury. An entrepreneur in the nineteenth century thought it sufficiently rich in iron to be worth exploiting and obtained a licence from a local landowner, but the iron content was not high enough to make the proposal economically viable, and it was never developed.[94]

Blind Lane continues through the medieval fields on the top of the hill and eventually leads into a different landscape of rough grass and quarrying. The transect cut by Blind Lane provides a good illustration of the geography of a fairly typical medieval farming system: arable fields cultivated in strips near the settlement, surrounded by an outfield of common uncultivated rough pasture. It does not require much imagination to visualise cattle being driven up the trackway from the village between arable strips, onto this wilder area *(89)*. There might have been small quarry pits open at the time; just beyond the cutting which takes the path onto the crest of the ridge there is a large quarry, long since abandoned, judging by the maturity of the soil and vegetation covering it.

90 Bronze Age barrows (1), a Second World War observation post (2), a Cold War Royal Observer Corps Post (3), Wears Hill, Abbotsbury

91 The entrance hatch (1), the ground zero indicator platform (2), the radiation monitoring probe tube (3), the ventilation shaft (4), Cold War ROC Post, Wears Hill

The coast path now turns west and passes south of four Bronze Age bowl barrows. There are two more at SY560862 *(90, 1)* which fall east and west of a roofless building and the brick base and concrete interior rendering suggest a Second World War date. The absence of embrasures suggest an observation post *(90, 2)*. Presumably, the construction of the upper part of the building in limestone is intended as camouflage. Immediately to the north-east of this site there is very good example of the surface indications of a Cold War Royal Observer Corps Post *(90, 3)*. Entrance hatch (blocked by concrete) *(91, 1)*, ground zero indicator platform *(91, 2)*, radiation monitoring probe tube *(91, 3)* and ventilation shaft, are visible *(91, 4)*[95].

Beyond the road the coast path enters the eastern end of Abbotsbury Castle Iron Age hillfort, first crossing the outer ditch and outer rampart, then skirting the inner ditch and inner rampart to gain the interior over the southern rampart. This approach, whilst avoiding the original entrance on the north-east, makes it easy to appreciate the contrast in scale of the south and east ramparts. This is likely to be a response to the gentle approach from the east, where the ramparts are high and ditches deep, and the steep approach from the south where ramparts and ditches are slight. The 'ditch' inside the eastern end is presumably a quarry to provide material for further heightening the inner rampart. On the west and north sides, this contrast between ridge and slope fortifications is repeated. A Bronze Age bowl barrow, one of the group first encountered on Wears Hill which existed before the hillfort was built, was enclosed by it ramparts *(92, 1)*. West of the barrow a substantial land boundary runs north-east – south-west across the site. This is later than the hillfort, as it cuts through its defences. Also later than the defences, for the same reason, is the 'L'-shaped bank and ditch enclosing a small space in the south-west corner of the site *(92, 2)*. It has been suggested that this might have been the site of a Roman military signalling station, but a small exploratory excavation failed to provide any evidence to support this.[96] Abbotsbury Castle is the only hillfort on the coast path which can be examined without restriction. It is worth taking advantage of this opportunity, as the site contains hut circles to the east of the land boundary which are identifiable on the ground. Ploughing has destroyed most surface evidence west of the land boundary. In its survey the Royal Commission on Historical Monuments plotted less than ten of these, to the north-east of the round barrow.[97] More recently, aerial photography has added a further 26 circular features, some probably pits, and some linear and rectangular features.[98]

To the north, another Iron Age hillfort, Eggardon, can be seen on a clear day *(93, 1)*. The defences at this site, as at Flowers Barrow, have been damaged by land slipping, but unlike Flowers Barrow the damage must have occurred during its occupation, as it has been repaired by the construction of new lengths of rampart.

The lower slopes on the north and south sides of the Abbotsbury Castle are very hummocky. This is a natural landform caused by the slumping of harder rocks over softer, more mobile clays beneath.

The path leaves Abbotsbury Castle in the south-west corner, crossing the road and continuing west, past three more round barrows, the last in the group on this ridge. The second of these has been damaged by a substantial trench, almost certainly the result of eighteenth- or nineteenth-century antiquarian digging for grave goods. In the infancy of archaeology as a discipline, this was the practice which gave rise to the carefully controlled and recorded excavation of today. An example of an antiquarian 'dig' was given at Hambury Tout.

Ahead on the Knoll is a building silhouetted against the sky *(94)*. This appears to have been a coastguard lookout or possibly a signalling station and stands on another Bronze Age barrow. Pottery found in this barrow was considered in the report of the excavation of three others nearby.[99] This illustrates the approach to barrow excavation in the mid-twentieth century, and makes an interesting contrast to the antiquarian approach just mentioned. One detail of this excavation has potentially wide implications – this was the presence in one of the barrows of a kerb of Quarr stone, which outcrops on the Isle of Wight, and shows that the stones must have been brought part of the way by boat. That is notable in its own right, as direct evidence for maritime transport is relatively rare from this time, perhaps around 1500 to 1200 BC, but even more interesting is what it might say about the conceptual world of the people who attached sufficient importance to these rocks or their associations to fetch them from so far away. A well-known analogy may be the transport of the blue stones to Stonehenge from Wales.

Half a kilometre south-east of the Knoll, an intriguing Romano-British site was excavated in the 1960s. Traditionally known as Walls, it was aptly named, as its main feature was a double enclosure of dry stone walling. This contained evidence of buildings which were impossible to

92 Bronze Age round barrow (1), enclosure (2), Abbotsbury Castle Iron Age Hillfort from the south-east

93 South Dorset Ridgeway from Abbotsbury Castle, with Eggardon Hillfort (1) on the skyline

94 The Knoll, Puncknowle, from the south-east

95 Kiln head and a pot of limekiln on Limekiln Hill, West Bexington

interpret with confidence, and copious artefacts which included: coarse and fine pottery vessels, quern stones and stone mortaria, coins, brooches, bronze spoons and bracelets, iron spearheads and a stylus, lead weights, bone pins, a gemstone from a ring with an engraving of Neptune, bracelets, spindle whorls and a platter of Kimmeridge shale and hundreds of hobnails. These features suggested an interpretation which went beyond simple domestic and farming activity, yet did not convincingly support a religious or ritual alternative.[100]

At SY540871, on Limekiln Hill, just before it turns south to West Bexington, the coast path crosses the low face of an old quarry which exploited the Forest Marble limestone just beneath the surface, and immediately south of the path is the reason for the quarrying: the limekiln. During the later eighteenth, the nineteenth and early twentieth centuries there was considerable demand for lime for agricultural improvement, in which it was used for the management of soil acidity, and as the binder in building mortar. Lime is calcium hydroxide and this is obtained by treating calcium oxide with water. Calcium oxide is obtained by decomposing calcium carbonate, and calcium carbonate is the main constituent of limestone. A limekiln is the reactor in which heat converted limestone into calcium oxide. Over 300 limekilns are known to have existed in Dorset,[101] most supplying local demand – their distribution adhering closely to sources of suitable limestone. Essentially a limekiln is a wide chimney (the pot) in which a mixture of broken limestone and fuel (usually some sort of coal) was burnt. The pot was constricted towards the bottom, where it was supported by an arch (the draw arch). Within this was the hearth (draw hole) where the fire was ignited and controlled, and through which the burnt lime was withdrawn. Above the draw arch there was usually a hole (the poking hole) used to monitor the progress of the reaction. This example on Limekiln Hill is the best on the coast. Although it is a reconstruction and, despite the poorly drained and overgrown lower levels, it is worth examining as it illustrates many of the characteristic features of small limekilns. It is set in a bank, with its top (the kiln head, *95*) level with the base of the quarry so that limestone and fuel could be easily fed into it. Commonly, a kiln would be fired continuously for several days and periodically recharged with rock and fuel as lime was drawn from the base. The draw arch *(96)* was usually protected by a roofed structure to give protection to the lime burner and the product; this has not been retained in this reconstruction.

96 Draw arch of limekiln on Limekiln Hill, West Bexington

Once back on the coastal path anyone feeling deprived of pillboxes will feel a sense of relief, as immediately west of the houses (SY531865) is another in the series guarding Chesil Beach from positions on the lower parts of slope to the north. Including this one, there are four between here and Burton Beach, a distance of about 4.5km. They are all in a roughly similar relationship to the topography and all appear to be hexagonal brick and concrete (Type 22), except the one on the hill overlooking Burton Beach from the east, which is square (Type 26). There are none between Burton Beach and West Bay, where the beach is backed by cliffs.

At SY522880 there is another clearly visible limekiln. The design is similar to that seen on Limekiln Hill above West Bexington.

Just beyond the tracks leading down to Cogden Beach, there is an abandoned coastguard lookout (SY502885) associated with coastguard houses behind the trees to the west.

Burton Cliff, west of Burton Beach, is mentioned in most guide books in connection with its use in 1944 in training the US Army 1st Infantry Division for its coming cliff assault on Omaha Beach in Operation Overlord. This ephemeral episode would not be expected to have left any traces, but there is a lot of evidence of Second World War occupation of the area apparent in a casual survey. This includes: a brick building with a blast protection wall in front of its door in the grounds of the isolated pink-washed cottage; another building of similar brick behind the Burton Cliff Hotel; footings of probable Second World War buildings on the east side of Burton Beach car park and at the foot of the cliff on the west of the beach; a brick building with concrete buttresses dug into the inner cliff just north of this point – this is in use as the Hive Ice Cream Parlour; a ring about 1m in diameter marked by large bolts (eight of about twenty are visible) in the footpath at SY488888, which is a holdfast for a coastal defence gun.

Looking east from Burton Cliff, the last in the series of pillboxes west of West Bexington can be seen *(97)*, with Blind Barrow behind it. There is some doubt about whether this is a barrow or a natural mound.[102] On the slope below and to the north there are traces of medieval strip lynchets. As the coast path rises onto Burton Cliff, contrast the dry stone walls here, which reflect the ready availability of stone, with the hedges which mark field boundaries on the slopes to the east, and in the valley to the north where suitable stone is not available nearby. These hedges are a reminder of the power and prevailing direction of the wind which can scour this coast, invoking an impression of people cowering for protection, their backs to its raw blast.

97 A Second World War Pillbox *(1)*, Burton Beach from the west

At SY485891 a prominent negative lynchet heads north from the cliff-edge (a seat has been placed on it) and turns west to join the field wall. Closer inspection suggests that the feature is a double lynchet with a slight hollow in between. If this is correct, it is probably a hollow way associated with the settlement of Southover, south of Burton Bradstock. Alongside the buildings mentioned in the next paragraph there is a terraced track sloping gently north-west, which is probably another defunct route connected with Southover.

As the path skirts inland at the western foot of Burton Cliff to seek a crossing of the river Bride, it passes the footings of five more Second World War buildings, one cut into the lower north-west facing slope, the others beside the track just before it crosses the stream: three of these are close together and the fourth is connected to the others by a concrete slab path. The secondary literature appears to be silent on these buildings and complex at Burton Beach, to which they may be related. The topic invites further research.

This concentration of Second World War remains encourages the thought that the roughly circular hollow on the western end of Burton Cliff (SY480890) may be associated with this activity, for example as temporary field works for a light gun or searchlight. However, more objectively the details do not support this interpretation – the lack of symmetry and the central mound (of spoil?) suggest a quarry. This interpretation is supported by the cliff section which shows a band of limestone aligned with the pit.

The skyline features on the cliff-edge looking north-west from Burton Freshwater suggest burial mounds, but on reaching the top it becomes clear that these are modern artefacts associated with the golf course. Some of these in the middle of the course look deceptively 'barrowish' and have potential, perhaps, for being noted by future field workers as 'previously unrecorded barrows' when currrent land use has long ceased.

WEST BAY TO GOLDEN CAP

An inland diversion to avoid unstable cliffs as it climbs north-west from West Bay takes the path over a circular terrace about 15m in diameter halfway up the slope. Its symmetry suggests a Second World War military

98 Limekiln, West Cliff, West Bay

earthwork, possibly the site of a gun emplacement. An emergency coast defence battery has been recorded at this location (SY 456906).[103]

There is a quarry beside the path where it turns westward and passes through a gate and, in it are the remains of a small limekiln *(98)*, enough of which remains to show that the draw arch is of conical form, similar to that seen near West Bexington.

The view ahead on the descent to Eype Mouth has Thorncombe beacon on the skyline, and the bracken-covered mound is one of the Bronze Age barrows which are sited there.

There are four tumbled Second World War anti-tank obstacles at the top of the beach at Eype Mouth, and on the east side of the stream a little to the north there is a brick and concrete Type 22 pillbox. At least two Dragon's Teeth survive at the mouth of the next stream to the west, at Sea Town.

At the summit of Thorncombe Beacon the cleft on the cliff-edge is the remnant of a small quarry which extended around the east side of the hill. There is a slight terrace beside it, which could have served to link it to the track leading down from the top of the ridge to the north east. The cliff section shows that the quarry was exploiting the angular gravel capping, probably for road surface metalling. There is also a slight lynchet below the track, about a third of the way down the hill, running around the south-east-facing slope, which is presumably the result of cultivation.

On a clear day it is possible to see Pilsdon Pen and Waddon Hill on the northern skyline, a little to the west and east respectively of the much pitted Quarry Hill in the foreground. The former is the site of Dorset's highest Iron Age hillfort, on which excavation has demonstrated the presence of round houses.[104] Attention has been drawn to the absence of evidence for grain storage in these excavations, and the possibility suggested, if this absence is real, that it may show that the occupants practiced pastoral rather than mixed arable farming.[105] On Waddon Hill there is the only certain Roman military site visible from the coast path. Here in the middle years of the first century AD, not long after the invasion, the Roman Army's Second Legion built and occupied a fort for troops, presumably controlling the recently subdued but potentially rebellious Durotrigians.

At the time of writing an excavation has just been completed by National Trust Archaeologists on the cliff-edge in anticipation of the loss of evidence to cliff erosion.[106] From previous finds there was an expectation of finding a Bronze Age site, but flints belonging to the Mesolithic and the Neolithic periods were discovered. Samples from a buried soil horizon were taken so that the pollen preserved from the time of burial could be analysed. The report of this study is not yet available, but an idea of the kind of information about the environment that might be obtained from the pollen evidence is described later in the context of an earlier excavation on the adjacent hill, Golden Cap.

As the coast path descends towards Sea Town on Ridge Cliff, it crosses a series of old field boundaries and an associated terraced track leading to them from the valley to the north-west *(99)*. The boundaries comprise a ditch and a bank (sometimes two banks with a ditch between) and when functional the banks would have carried a hedge. Erosion on the path has revealed the interiors of some of the banks and show that some contained a rubble core and others earth. This probably reflects the variability in the material dug from the ditches. At some time these fields must have been ploughed, as their upper and lower boundaries are marked by lynchets caused by soil movement down slope.

These fields tend to be square as opposed to elongated: 'squarish' fields have elsewhere been classified as 'celtic' fields. Why are these not celtic fields? Principally, because they are too 'fresh', too sharp and well defined, insufficiently weathered to be prehistoric and they are also

99 A Field system, Sea Town

bigger than most prehistoric fields. A better view of the pattern of these fields is to be had from Golden Cap and that is a more convenient place to consider their date.

View Point Golden Cap

Golden Cap is noted for its stunning views from Portland Bill *(colour plate 16)* to Lyme Regis and beyond *(100)* and, from here the general pattern of settlements and field boundaries in the area are spread out to the north *(101)*. This landscape is rather different from that seen further to the east; it is one of isolated small farms. Near the settlements the fields tend to be small and irregular (this is especially so in the case of the older settlements). The boundaries are all thick hedges and in this area they are functional as the National Trust has a policy of management to maintain this traditional pattern, which has its origins in the early medieval period or before. In its early form, there were fewer settlements surrounded by small groups of irregular fields; these would have been gradually supplemented by woodland clearance.

127

100 The landscape west of Golden Cap

101 The landscape north-west of Golden Cap

1 A rifle range butt with an Ordnance Survey triangulation station in the foreground, Ballard Down

2 Circular earthwork, Ballard Down. See text for possible interpretations

3 Looking east across the quarried landscape and a restored stone mine, Durlston

4 A restored stone mine entrance, Durlston

5 The signal station enclosure, Durlston

6 Alan Williams Turret, Seacombe

7 Medieval strip lynchets, East Man, Winspit

8 Clavel's Hard from the east

9 North Egliston is the settlement on the right; the estate boundary between Tyneham and North Egliston, which is of Saxon date, can be seen crossing the picture diagonally from the bottom left, Tyneham valley

10 Flowers Barrow Iron Age hillfort at the highest point on the cliff, and a Romano-British occupation site on the cliff-edge above the dense scrub, Worbarrow bay

11 Bindon Hill and Lulworth Bay from the west: western cross-contour rampart on the facing slope, traces of lower western defences south of the village

12 A Second World War obseravtion post, Upton Fort

13 Upton Fort from the west

14 Observation posts near the Verne, Portland

15 A Second World War observation post near Blacknor Fort, and to its left a possible pre-war rocket-testing launch site

16 The landscape east of Golden Cap

In the post-medieval period, clearance became much more extensive and enclosures formed the larger more regular fields which can be seen further away from the settlements. It is to this period that the abandoned enclosures east of Seatown probably belong. There is an important environmental factor associated with the difference in settlement development between eastern and western Dorset. In the west, underlying rocks tend to produce clay rich soils, which do not drain easily. They readily become waterlogged (gleyed) and it is difficult to grow arable crops on them. Farmers were reluctant to remove the natural woodland from these soils and, when they did, tended to put them to their best use, pasture.

This is also the location of an interesting excavation by Martin Papworth in 1992. A group of probable Bronze Age barrows occur near the cliff-edge and it was decided that the one most at risk from cliff erosion should be excavated and recorded. A trench was dug across the mound, revealing details of its construction and also an old ground surface on which there was a deposit of charcoal, probably associated with funerary ritual, possibly a pyre. Among the finds there were no pottery or bones (the latter would be unlikely to have survived in the acid burial conditions); the single flint implement found is probably of Early Bronze Age date. Samples of the soil and charcoal were taken – the soil for the extraction and study of pollen grains,[107] the charcoal for radio-carbon dating.[108] The radiocarbon dates indicated that the barrow was constructed in around 2000 BC. Interpretation of the pollen evidence suggested that oak woodland with an under storey of holly and hazel was the dominant vegetation at the time the barrow was built, and also the possibility that this may have been the product of woodland regenera-tion after earlier clearance. The presence of this woodland can be taken as an indication of relatively low population density in the western part of Dorset, either not yet having cleared woodland or not having main-tained earlier deforestation. It is consistent with the low density of burial monuments of the period, west of the South Dorset Ridgeway. There is no direct evidence from this excavation to date the woodland clearance that later took place. The excavators were inclined to assume that, on the hilltop at least, clearance occurred not long after the barrow was built, on the grounds that the barrow would have been invisible from the surrounding area if built in woodland, which would contradict the generally held opinion that barrows were sited to be widely visible.

The excavation also showed that the mound had been disturbed when the base of a signalling tower was inserted in it. Documentary evidence dated this activity to between 1798 and 1814 and linked it to the threat of Napoleonic invasion and the raising of a corps of Sea Fencibles, to man a series of signalling stations watching the coast. Three of these were discussed earlier at Ballard Down, Round Down, and White Nothe. After 1814, this station was replaced by another signalling station a little to the north-east. Earthworks associated with these can be seen about 30m north–north-east of the Earl of Antrim memorial.

The report of this excavation[109] can be read as an example of the late twentieth-century approach to barrow excavation and can be compared with those cited earlier, noting the application of scientific techniques to dating and the gathering of environmental data.

GOLDEN CAP TO STONEBARROW HILL AND LYME REGIS

A short detour from the coast path as it traverses the lower ground between Golden Cap and Stonebarrow Hill provides close encounters with the managed field boundaries and with one of the early settlements, Stanton St Gabriel. There is a ruined chapel here, of which parts of the walls of the chancel, nave and south porch survive, but there is insufficient architectural detail to secure its original date, which is probably twelfth century. To the south of the chapel, near the surviving buildings, there are slight earthworks suggesting that the earlier settlement was more extensive and has since shrunk.

Returning to the coast path and starting the climb to Stonebarrow Hill, just west of Westhay Water (SY386926) there is an embanked enclosure, the south-east corner of which is strengthened with mortared chert blocks *(102)*. Its interior appears hollow, though undergrowth makes this difficult to examine, and there is a gully emerging from its north-east corner. Superficially, its appearance might suggest a defensive function, but its form does not match any familiar category. The condition of the mortared stones suggests some age, perhaps a century. This is about as far as field inference can go, but early Ordnance Survey maps show a limekiln in this position.[110]

At Westhay Farm, notice the rectangular earthwork platforms to the south of the present farmyard. As at Stanton St Gabriel, this is an indi-

102 A limekiln near Westhay Water

cation of earlier abandoned settlement at the site. There was a radar station near this location operating until the 1960s, but all that remains is the occasional concrete fence post. The National Trust centre at the top of the hill has more tangible radar associations. The shop and hostel are housed in an original building which was part of a Rotor early warning system operating between 1954 and 1974. Around it in the partly original enclosure there are footings of other buildings.

At Stonebarrow Hill, on the cliff overlooking Cain's Folly, this guide almost completes its task. There are still 5km before the western boundary of the Dorset Coast is reached at Lyme Regis, but much of this is urban settlement and, from this point, at the time of writing, the coast path had been diverted onto inland roads to avoid the pronounced and active cliff erosion which has carried away the former cliff path. The severity of the erosion is well seen from this point. *Approach the cliff-edge with the greatest care.*

Caught up in this geological instability are the final (and almost terminal) sites – one here and the other on the west side of the landslip

103 Second World War coastal defence radar buildings, Cains Folly, Charmouth

104 A Second World War gun battery, Timber Hill, Lyme Regis.

at Timber Hill. Below, in the undercliff are the remains of two Second World War radar buildings *(103)*. Originally set on the cliff top to function as a coastal defence radar station, they slipped down the cliff in 1942. The site on Timber Hill, which can be reached from the coast path detour at SY345936, was a coastal defence gun battery built in 1942.[111] It survives as part of the camouflage wall of one of the gun housings and a few concrete hut bases set on terraces above the remains of the old track. Much of the operational part of the site has already been carried away and the most easterly buildings are in the zone of active cliff movement *(104)*.

Perhaps it is fitting that we began and ended with archaeological sites from the Second World War. Sites of that period probably outnumber those of any other and it was one of our aims to be representative. We also intended to concentrate on the lesser known and neglected sites: those from the Second World War demonstrably belong to that category. They also illustrate too well, despite the impregnability of many of them, their vulnerability, not just to coastal erosion but to the decay which threatens any element of the heritage which is accorded a low score in the changing value judgements we make about the past. These sites, so close in time yet in some ways so obscure, also make a special plea for further research. Unlike sites of earlier times, we can still talk to people about how these sites functioned, what social practices were associated with them and what they meant to them personally. But that research must be done now: soon those memories will be extinguished and it will be too late.

Two

CHRONOLOGICAL OUTLINE

Travelling along the Dorset coast, we have encountered archaeological sites of many periods but in chronological disorder. This section, in chronological order, is a much simplified summary of the influences that human beings have had on the natural landscape and the main developments in the built environment of the region; it includes cross-references to many of the sites discussed in the guide.

Although human activity on what is now the Dorset Coast begins very much earlier, the first people of which there is evidence were those living during the warming climate after the last Ice Age. These Mesolithic[1] people adapted their way of life to hunting and gathering in the largely forested environment which developed after about 9000 BC. They are not notable for their additions to the built landscape, but the pollen record in buried sediments (pp. 18, 129) shows that they began to clear woodland to encourage grass growth and concentrate grazing animals, such as deer, to improve their hunting. In some areas of poorer soils these clearances may have persisted to influence the landscape of today. Mesolithic sites were encountered at Portland (p. 99) and on the Fleet (p. 109). Here the coastline is still reasonably close to its position in about 6000 BC and the exploitation of coastal resources played a part in this diversified economy.

The Mesolithic hunting and gathering economy gave way to farming not long after 4000 BC. Important elements of farming technology certainly came from mainland Europe, from which Britain was by now separated by the English Channel, but it is not clear whether the local population adopted farming or whether they died out along with their traditional way of life. A major environmental impact of early Neolithic farming was the clearance of woodland on at least the lighter and more fertile soils to provide land for arable cultivation, and grazing of domesticated animals, mainly cattle and sheep.

It was also in the early Neolithic that human beings, for the first time, built additional deliberate landscape features. The most important of these are long barrows and Causewayed Enclosures: both seem to be concerned with death and social ritual. Long barrows were massive mounds of earth, usually containing wood or stone 'chambers', built in prominent positions on the landscape. An almost universal feature is that the chambers contain remains of the dead. Often many individuals are present and commonly these are represented by only a few bones. In the case of the wooden chambered tombs (earthen long barrows), the bones usually seem to have been accumulated and brought together in the final act of constructing the tomb; the stone chambered tombs often seem to have been accessible for a long time after building, but seem to have accumulated bones in a similar way. Tomb building seems to have been a communal activity, and one in which the activities of individuals or small groups appears to be recognisable. The location of long barrows and the investment of communal resources in their building is currently thought by many prehistorians to amount to the making of territorial statements, or claims, in most cases reinforced by symbolic references to ancestral rights and customs in the bones they contain.

Long barrows tend to occur in clusters. In Dorset there is a cluster on the South Dorset Ridgeway near Dorchester, and another on Cranborne Chase. Associated with these clusters, which presumably identify concentrations of settlement, is the other type of landscape feature – the Causewayed Enclosure. That linked to the South Dorset Ridgeway cluster was on the hill occupied much later by the Iron Age hillfort, Maiden Castle; that belonging to Cranborne Chase is in similar relationship to a later hillfort on Hambledon Hill. Causewayed Enclosures were areas of many hectares enclosed by banks (possibly defensive during some periods of their existence) and discontinuous ditches. It does not appear that these sites were settled as permanent 'villages', but that they served as gathering places for dispersed communities, who used them periodically for ceremonial and social purposes. Rituals involving the deliberate burial of materials in the ditches seem to have been important and, at Hambledon Hill at least, there is strong evidence that corpses were exposed there after death, perhaps as part of the collection of ancestral remains for eventual burial in long barrows.

Also belonging to the centuries around 3000 BC is an uncommon class of sites which may be the boldest of all landscape statements in prehistory: cursus monuments. These are rectangular enclosures a few tens of metres wide, but up to several miles long and, apparently associated with the rituals embracing long barrows.

The closest approach to these fascinating sites that the coastal strip permits is the long barrow on Ailwood Down, which can be seen from Round Down near Durlston (p. 27), unless the speculation about a remnant of a possible Causewayed Enclosure on the cliff-edge near Worbarrow (p. 67) is allowed. The are several long barrows, including some very long examples (bank barrows) near the inland route of the coast path on the South Dorset Ridgeway, and a cursus (only visible in aerial photographs) near the Martin's Down bank barrow, Long Bredy.

Towards the middle of the third millennium BC, the significance attached to building long barrows and Causewayed Enclosures seems to have weakened, though those in existence still seem to have been respected and involved in ritual. Beginning to appear at this time – the late Neolithic, and continuing to do so for the next 500 years or so, were other important constructions which made an impact on the landscape. Among these were circular embanked enclosures known as henge monuments. Henge monuments varied widely in size and design. Some of the largest, of which there are examples at Knowlton on Cranborne Chase, and Mount Pleasant near Dorchester, contained very large timber buildings and remains of pottery and animal bones which are quite different from those found in the earlier Causewayed Enclosures. Timber circles are sometimes found inside henges or associated with them; later features in stone, and free-standing stone circles, begin to appear in the landscape, becoming particularly important in the years around 2000 BC. Stone circles varied in size too, and also in shape and complexity and, in these, as in the smaller henges, it is difficult to see anything but ritual motivation. To say these sites impacted on the landscape is not enough: henges, stones, landscape features and celestial phenomena were intimately bound in complex symbolic statements. We may be seeing the origins of a 'priestly' class in the special pottery and food remains associated with these sites. Regrettably, none of these later Neolithic and early Bronze Age ritual sites are encountered on the coastal strip, but their influences are not far away on the South Dorset Ridgeway. Besides Mount Pleasant, there is a huge timber circle and Maumbury Rings henge at Dorchester. There are stone circles at Winterborne Abbas and Kingston Russell, and an isolated example at Rempstone, about 5km west of Studland.

Forest clearance had continued throughout the Neolithic, and by the time of the great henges there is evidence for soil exhaustion and woodland regeneration in some areas. It is likely that exploitation of some valley soils was increasing by the end of the third millennium. The social and ideological changes implied by the diminishing significance of long barrows begin to be expressed in a new form of burial ritual at about this time. In bold contrast to the pooling of ancestral power in the long arrows, the significance of individual power is emphasised in the round barrows of the early Bronze Age. Not only are presumably high status individuals singled out in death, they are also accompanied in death by material goods, a practice rarely found earlier in the Neolithic. This package of symbols in the burial ritual: individual interment, absence of de-fleshing, the presence of fine pottery, flint and for the first time metal (copper or the earliest bronze) and a distinctive *round* burial mound speaks of a society in which individual power in life was a key to social control and identity. These round burial mounds, Bronze Age round barrows, are well represented near the coast. Examples are seen at a distance from Round Down (p. 27), Emmett's Hill (p. 38) and Redcliff Point (p. 82), and close by, for example at Bindon Hill (p. 68), Hambury Tout (p. 71), and near Abbotsbury Castle (p. 117). The contents and typology of round barrows are mentioned on pp. 71, 118 and 129.

By about 1500 BC, there has been a shift from the burial of the fresh corpse to the incorporation of cremated remains, often in pots (urns), in barrows. Urned cremation continues to be important for the next few hundred years, but its association with barrows wanes and barrow building largely ceases. So too does the ostentatious ritual manipulation of landscape in stone circle building. Spiritual interests begin to be directed down from the sky into the earth and water and ritual activity leaves little impact on the landscape of today. The Bronze Age landscape now begins to acquire an essentially domestic complexion.

For generations, settlements had been surrounded by recognisable arable fields, but it was not until the later Bronze Age that the agricultural landscape is organised on a scale and with enough stability to produce patterns of land boundaries and field systems and, occasionally the earthworks of their associated farms, durable enough to survive to this day. In many cases systems of 'celtic' fields more readily associated with Iron Age sites probably originated in the late Bronze Age and continued in use into the Romano-British period. Field systems such as these are seen on the coast at Handfast Point (p. 15), St Aldhelm's Head (p. 37), at Worbarrow Bay (p. 64) and in the coombes between Lulworth and White Nothe (p. 72). The best examples are on Kingston Down (p. 41) where the method of ploughing with an ard, which is thought to have created the distinctive 'squareness' of celtic fields, is discussed.

Whilst the agricultural landscape of the first millennium BC may have been relatively stable, there is social and ideological change expressed through elements of material culture – tools and pots. In particular there appears to be a growing tendency towards the expression of tension and conflict, and from about 500 BC this extends to another phase of ostentatious landscape modification, comparable in terms of the energy invested, to the building of Causewayed Enclosures, large henges and stone circles. But now the motivation is warfare and the manifestation the hillfort. There are over thirty Iron Age hillforts in Dorset. Two, Flower's Barrow (p. 64) and Abbotsbury Castle (p. 117), are crossed by the coast path, three if the hill-top enclosure, Bindon Hill (p. 68), is included. Three more, Chalbury (p. 82), Eggardon (p. 118) and Pilsdon Pen (p. 126), can be seen in the distance. Hillforts, many of which become increasingly formidable over time, are systems of deep ditches and massive banks. These usually surrounded an area between a few to several tens of hectares on a defensible steep-sided hilltop and were provided with strong gated entrances. Some hillforts contain evidence of intensive settlement: house sites, grain storage pits and granaries, while others show relatively little signs that they were much occupied. Whether the warfare which lay behind hillforts was hot or cold is debatable. Certainly, in some examples large hoards of pebbles have been found, which are thought to be sling projectiles, and the design of the ramparts in the later Iron Age has been said to give strategic advantage to defending slingers, but like the massive gates and daunting earthworks, these can be seen as deterrence in the absence of evidence for action which is not commonly demonstrated by excavation.

Whatever the functions of hillforts, they did not survive the Roman Conquest in the years following AD 43. Although this event may have been socially disruptive for some of the local hillfort occupants, its impact on the landscape was relatively slight. A Roman military presence was established for a few years to control the difficult Durotriges. This took the form of forts near Wimborne, inside the hillfort at Hod Hill and, in the west at Waddon Hill; the latter can be glimpsed from the coast (p. 126). Towns were founded, most obviously at Dorchester, and good straight roads cut through the prehistoric landscape, pointedly disregarding its old symbols, as at Oakley Down. Farming continued pretty much unchanged for a while, but eventually rectangular buildings replaced round ones, and baths and mosaic floors appeared in quite low status farms; villas represented high status land holding and estate management. Much of this is invisible in the modern landscape because, with the exception of roads, it has been overwritten by later activity. References to domestic sites reflecting these aspects of continuity and change are made at Emmett's Hill (p. 38) and Hounstout (p. 43). The tension and fusion of Iron Age and Roman ideologies find one expression in Romano-British religious sites. Romano-Celtic temples often demonstrate an ambiguity which opposes or combines classical architecture and Celtic ritual, a Roman deity and a Celtic god. This is illustrated at Jordan Hill (p. 84).

Perhaps the most striking result of the Roman occupation, again invisible in the landscape today, is found in the 'industrial' response of communities, particularly in the Isle of Purbeck, to the market opportunities which developed as a consequence. This is demonstrated by the expansion in the production of Black burnished ware pottery around the shores of Poole Harbour (p. 20) and, the exploitation of Purbeck marble (pp. 21, 63) and Kimmeridge shale (p. 47).

The Romano-British economy was in decline by the beginning of the fifth century AD, but it is likely that this did not mark any major changes in the pattern of land use. During the Saxon period, documents relating to land holding become increasingly informative and by the early medieval period many of the major land divisions which still survive appear to have been established. This is illustrated in the Tyneham valley (p. 61ff).

By the twelfth or thirteenth century, many of the hamlets and villages which still survive, as well as those which developed into larger settlements and those which declined or were deserted, had been established; some of them may have had continuous links with very much earlier times. Those which continued in some way to the present day have been excluded from this guide, but the essential part they play in giving the landscape its general character should not be overlooked. Here we have chosen to concentrate on the deserted settlements and the evidence of medieval activity which survives as relics in the landscape. Field systems associated with arable farming are the most common feature in the east of the region. Some time after the Romano-British period and by the early medieval period, changes in land tenure, agricultural management and the technology of ploughing had resulted in land around hamlets and villages, especially in the east of the region, being cultivated in groups of long narrow strips. Where these were extended under conditions of rising population and stagnant farming methods, to often difficult land that was to become marginal, they often survive as strip lynchets. There are several examples along the coast, the best being at Winspit, where farming methods are considered in more detail (p 33), and at Abbotsbury (p. 115). The landscape on the heavier land to the west, with its emphasis on pastoral farming, shows fewer of these features, but the gradual evolution of the present patterns of enclosure through successive encroachments on woodland is well seen from Golden Cap (p. 127). There is a deserted medieval village at Ringstead (p. 75) and comments are made at that point on the phenomenon generally. Evidence for shrunken and shifted settlement is noted at East Fleet (p. 110), Stanton St Gabriel (p. 130) and Westhay Farm, and at Tyneham (p. 61) where the demise had rather different causes.

If the broadly stable pattern of settlement established by the medieval period endows the landscape with a special character, then it is the buildings which fine tune this and modulate it with echoes of social and architectural change over time. Most ecclesiastical, administrative, and domestic buildings have not been included in this guide, not because they are unimportant, but because they are within settlements which have been omitted, they are still in use or re-use, or they are so important that they have their own guides or interpretations. The exceptions are two ruined castles of different date and purpose, Rufus (p. 96) and Sandsfoot (p. 85) a ruined church, St Andrews, Portland (p. 96) and a ruined chapel at Stanton St Gabriel (p. 130).

During the last three or four hundred years, changes in farming practice, beginning with the enclosures of open fields and common land and continuing to the ploughing of downland, hedge removal and 'set-aside' of more recent times, has had a profound effect on landscape. Enclosure is touched on (p. 62) but the later developments, except in so far as they affect the archaeological heritage (e.g. p. 19), receive little attention, as they are a feature of current land use.

Abandonment, disuse and neglect relate much more to military and industrial activity in the last few centuries, and it is these themes which dominate the archaeology of the last hundred years or so in this guide. Perhaps the remains of stone quarrying has had the biggest impact on the coastal landscape, particularly in the east of the region. Its effects are discussed at Durlston (p. 22ff) and Winspit (p. 29ff), and at various points on Portland (pp. 97-98) (p. 103ff). Even west of Portland, where large scale stone quarrying is rare, limekilns exploiting quarried limestone are encountered near West Bexington (p. 121 and p. 122), and at West Bay (p. 125). Bituminous shale quarrying and its use as a fuel and chemical feedstock is discussed at Kimmeridge (p. 53ff), and an aborted attempt to quarry iron stone at Abbotsbury is mentioned (p. 115). Evidence for the technology of quarrying and stone preparation is encountered at most of these locations, and artefacts associated with the shipping of stone by sea are seen at Winspit (p. 29) and Portland (p. 97). Features associated with the transport of stone within quarries are noted at Portland, where there are fine examples of bridgework (p. 104) and fascinating details of tramways to be seen (pp. 99, 103). These are very early examples of the development of railway transport, and some archaeological features of the line which eventually connected them to the mainland are noted near Ferry Bridge (p. 86).

Military archaeology probably accounts for the largest number of sites on the Dorset Coast and, those from the Second World War greatly outnumber those of earlier periods. The twelfth-century Rufus Castle and the sixteenth-century Sandsfoot Castle guarding Portland Harbour have already been mentioned, and Portland Castle should be associated with the latter. The nineteenth century saw coastal defence forts and gun batteries at Upton (p. 79), The Nothe (p. 85), The Verne (p. 88), and also on Portland the High Angle Battery (p. 88), East Weares Battery (p. 92), and Blacknor Fort (p. 101), most of which were modified for twentieth-century use. The threat of Napoleonic invasion also led to the signal stations manned by the Sea Fencibles which have been noted at Ballard Down (p. 17), Round Down (p. 23), White Nothe (p. 75) and Golden Cap (p. 130).

Various elements of Second World War defence activity transformed the landscape of the Dorset coast in the detail. A lot of this survives, though it must be a small fraction of what there was originally and much of it is now in a poor state of preservation. There are traces of several sites connected with military training: the air-to-ground firing range represented by buildings at Ballard (p. 16), the artillery range near Kimmeridge (p. 50), the more specialised preparations for D-Day at Studland, symbolised by Fort Henry (p. 14) and rifle ranges at Ballard (p. 16), Portland (p. 92) and Little Sea (p. 110).

Watching the sky and the sea were radar stations and there is field evidence at St Aldhelm's Head (p. 34), Ringstead (p. 77), Portland (pp. 91, 92 and 104) and Cain's Folly (p. 131). Hounstout, the site at which vital developments in the science and technology of radar between 1940 and 1942 is mentioned (p. 41).

Defending the sky from the ground were anti-aircraft gun batteries: one can be seen from a distance at Portland (p. 88). The coast was defended at long range by coastal gun batteries. In addition to the re-equipped forts mentioned above, there are remains of these at Studland (p. 14), Swanage (p. 21), Burton Cliff (p. 123), West Bay (p. 125) and Timber Hill (p. 133). There are observation posts, most presumably connected with gunnery, at Kimmeridge (p. 50), Flowers Barrow (p. 64), White Nothe (p. 73), Upton (p. 79), Portland (p. 102) and Abbotsbury (p. 117).

Preparation for defence against an invasion of Britain is reflected in anti-tank blocks at several places, those at Studland (p. 13), Worbarrow (p. 63) and Abbotsbury (p. 112) being the best preserved groups. It is also evident in the putative anti-glider defences on Bindon Hill (p. 69) and the pillboxes. Examples of the latter are encountered on every low-lying stretch of coast from Studland to Sea Town. They must outnumber any other type of site of any period. There are too many to cross-reference here, but a few warrant special mention: the uncommon Allen-Williams turret (pp. 28 and 64), an example with anti-ricochet walls (p. 109), an example with additional camouflage (e.g. p. 110), and one with a readable graffito (p. 111). A comment on typology and construction of pillboxes is included on p. 57.

Most recently the Cold War left a faint imprint on the Dorset coast in the form of two Royal Observer Corps posts at Portland (p. 100) and Abbotsbury (p. 117), rotor radar stations at Ringstead (p. 78), Portland (p. 91) and Stonebarrow Hill (p. 131), and the tropospheric scatter communications site at Ringstead (p. 79).

APPENDIX

This book tries to understand *things* in the landscape, a process which is not as simple as it might seem. The general problem concerns how the material world means something to us, or how we impose meaning upon it and, what it is like to say that we understand some element of the material world, particularly when that element survives from the past. Among the various instances of the material world we might consider, the most important class for field archaeologists is that which implies definitions of space, for example enclosures like: sheds, fields, churches, houses and quarries, and roads and railways which can be thought of as very long, narrow enclosures.

No doubt you will have associated these nouns with different things or classes of things. This is not to say that the nouns are *things*, nor that each of us associate a noun with the exact same thing in the world, but I do not want to pursue the matter from the point of view of what *words* mean. After all, there is not much language, or indeed conscious thought, involved in the act of spearing a piece of food with a fork and putting it into our mouth. Nor is there in the wider sense of 'fork' which makes us use it with a knife, at a table at something we call a meal. These interactions with the material world we will loosely call *social practice* and it is that, and the meaning things have in that context, which I want to explore. Of course, we need words to describe meanings and social practice involving things, but words are not primary. Things, and how we behave with them, are.

If you were shown a small wooden building with a bituminous felt roof, no windows and padlocked door, standing on breeze blocks at the bottom of a domestic garden, you would use 'shed' if you wanted to communicate you understood what the thing was to the person describing it. But what is really in 'sheddiness'? In one sense there are only unique sheds: in one there will be tools neatly stored; in another there are tools and paint pots, and behind them a box with a cushion on which the controller of this space (are sheds male domains?) goes for a smoke – an inappropriate activity in the 'living space' a few metres away; in a third there is a complex model railway layout; the fourth is entered with trepidation when that elusive object cannot be found, and the quest involves turning out the heap of disordered junk that has found its way to this depository – a kind of purgatory before the final act of disposal. Then there are sheds which have a more independent existence on allotments, surrogate dwellings with territorial pretensions; there are others near the shore, along with others in miniature communities, their territories defined by beach boulders, each with an astonishing price tag. One person's shed may be another person's beach hut – from this variability we can extract a general sense of 'sheddiness' which is complex in its implications of social practice. This is the rather vague sense of shed we all share; the more specialised social implications of the beach hut are known to smaller groups; and there is the shed in your own garden, which only you are familiar with in all its functional and emotional nuances.

To formalise: In thinking about sheds we seem to imply the possession of a hierarchy of concepts which in order of increasing particularity are something like: an idea of space, an idea of a boundary defining a particular bit of space, an idea of a shed in general, an idea of specialised sheds, an idea of a particular shed.

These concepts become increasingly more specific, and at the same time are shared by a decreasing group of people. Everybody has some sense of space: what counts as a boundary probably differs between large cultural groups (for example, indigenous Australians conceive boundaries quite differently from Western Europeans), the garden shed may be particularly British, the beach hut will be construed with subtle differences by different beach hut communities, and the group sharing the meaning attached to the shed in your garden is very limited. 'Shed' is a continuum of meaning and social practice generally and widely shared at one end, very personal and unique at the other, and thus it is with any element of the material world we can think of.

There is another dimension to be considered, which concerns the detail or richness of meaning, and to appreciate how complex this is in our own case requires thoughtful reflection, because we do not usually notice it. Think about a domestic dwelling. Most people in the 'developed world' do not have the least difficulty in behaving 'normally' in someone else's house. On calling they are not surprised to enter by the 'front' door rather than the 'back', to be shown into the lounge (normally they would be surprised by being entertained in the bedroom); they are not surprised at a meal being cooked in the kitchen (but a cooker in the bathroom would be odd). In the lounge they would not 'naturally' sit on the television, or be handed coffee in a flower vase, nor would they be puzzled by photographs on the mantelpiece. This merely touches the surface of the detail that could be described in general, to say nothing of the level of detail you could set out in the case of your own home, which would include a wealth of emotional connections with objects such as souvenirs and photographs. Yet it seems so silly to describe this, because we all 'know' it without thinking and what we know without thinking is encyclopaedic. How does it come about that we deal so easily and unconsciously in such a complex way with our material world? We somehow just socialise ourselves into it through a long childhood in a complex social and material environment. To become socialised is to become materialised. To function with social competence is as much about knowing how to do things with knives, forks, mobile phones, mobile libraries, taxis and cinemas, as it is – I was going to say – as knowing how to interact with people, but it is just about impossible to think of a way of interacting with other people which does not involve material culture too. In this rich environment with its complex shades of meanings and practices, and levels of generalisation, where does the truth about it all lie? Could it be described truthfully? It depends what you mean by truth. There are probably generalisations that we would all agree on and therefore be prepared to call 'true' but, as the account becomes more and more personal, the increasing uniqueness of perspective makes agreement less and less likely, even in the complete absence of dissimulation.

This gets us to the problem of the past: we want to understand the past and to make true statements about it. To talk about our own society in its material world, or the material world in our own society, is to assume rich knowledge – some of which is widely shared, some restricted, and some secretly personal – an acquaintance that we get by living in the world adapting to the emergence of new objects,[1] conceptually adjusting to obsolescence. What about past societies and their knowledge? And how could we know when we are talking 'truthfully' about them? One extreme view is to say that we cannot 'know' the past in the sense we apply 'know' to our own material world. We must just accept that all that can be said about the past is more or less fictional. Another extreme approach, at first sight more positive, is to say that our own acquaintance with the material world can be projected back onto the past, somehow revealing how it was. After all, some of the material world of the past is here with us in museums and in the landscape – surely we can operate on it in the present, can't we? Well, we can *describe* in the present – measure it, do scientific analysis on it – but to use it as a means of time travel is not possible: the past *social context* is no longer with us, its objects are isolated, marooned, out of context, and what they mean to us now *cannot* be what they meant in the past. Think of the flat iron: today we might encounter it rusting in a junk shop for £12 (a collectable), beside the kitchen door (a door stop), with fire irons beside a gas fire in the lounge (retro-décor), or in a 1900 kitchen diorama in a museum (theatre). In the life of the Victorian housemaid its meaning would probably have involved long hours of drudgery, a hot steaming laundry room and a kitchen range in which a flat iron was part of a series with different weights for different jobs, and replicated to ensure there was a hot one ready (and she would know when it was ready when a ball of saliva would run around it when spat on) when the one you were using cooled down. I have cheated in this example, because it is easy to create a scenario with a flat iron which seems plausible, as Victorian society was not that different from our own. Was it? I hope you did not believe my assertion, or were taken in by my fiction! But in case you did or were, think about a Bronze Age round barrow on a chalk ridge, inside, the crouched skeleton with beaker, dagger and …. What could anyone say about the 'meaning' and social practices associated with that, that carried anything like the richness and subtlety I have been attaching to the 'meaning' of material culture in our own social context? The further back you go, the more obvious are the flaws in the 'projection' approach to understanding past material culture.

It is generally agreed we must not lose sight of these limitations, but most archaeologists and historians would not accept that they prevent anything worthwhile from being done, possibly because this would render illegitimate their whole enterprise. One way of trying to work around the dilemma is indicated by the word I carefully inserted in the sentence beginning 'The Victorian housemaid…' – *probably*. Along with 'probably' are 'might', 'possibly', 'could have been', 'may', 'may well have', 'it is likely that', 'appears to be', 'seems', and all those other expressions we use to denote various levels of uncertainty (an optimist would say 'certainty'). These are probably the most useful words in the vocabulary of those trying to talk about the past. I use them extensively here.

But I cannot pretend I am convinced that this really solves the problem of the past material world remaining essentially fictional. Even carefully qualified 'certainties' will usually be the result of other judgements based on the balancing of probabilities. The longer these chains of reasoning are, the more likely the conclusion will be insecure, and the weaker the claim to knowledge will be. Perhaps we should be honest and admit to fiction and simply try to construct it as rigorously as we can, supporting it with opinion-free rational argument, as far as that can be based on opinion, based on sound, critically scrutinised evidence, and to make clear the level of generalisation (shared meaning) we are trying to achieve – almost inevitably very wide in the remoter past, perhaps very narrow when we are using living memory as evidence. Perhaps we have to accept this as the closest approach we can make.

There is a trap lying in wait for those who take a particularly thorough approach to the past, who commendably absorb the entire primary and secondary information until their grasp of it is unassailable. There is a sense of achievement in reaching this position and it is easy to mistake a command of these sources for knowledge of the past. It is so easy, that it is possible to lose sight of the slippery quarry, knowledge of the past itself, and to suppose it lies in the virtuosity of source criticism and exposition, and its weaving into the 'knowledge' enshrined in the community of contemporary scholarship.

Where does this guide stand in relation to understanding the past? At the very beginning. It is mostly concerned with observation of the material past in the present. It makes only the broadest generalisations, and I am usually prepared to be satisfied when I have fitted the observation into the 'knowledge community' to which I feel I belong.

NOTES

ONE: ARCHAEOLOGY ON THE DORSET
COAST

1   Any feature which appears to result
    from human activity, which is no
    longer functional, and which an
    archaeologist would want to
    understand and include in an
    interpretation of the landscape will
    be treated as an 'archaeological
    problem'. What it is like to claim
    something is understood in
    archaeology is discussed further in
    the Appendix

2   A useful introduction to some
    Second World War sites in Dorset is
    Pomeroy 1995, and to field remains
    in general from this period, Brown *et
    al.*, 1995

3   'Context' includes not only the
    spatial relationship between an
    artefact and its landscape and other
    objects of relevance, but also how it
    was embedded in the social practices
    and understandings of its time. From
    another perspective there is the
    context in the 'mind' of the
    interpreter: a person with much
    experience and knowledge of filled
    archaeology is more likely to
    'understand' an artefact than
    someone just beginning

4   Pomeroy, 1995, 78

5   Pomeroy, 1995, 94

6   Ordnance Survey 1:25000
    Pathfinder Series, Sheet SY
    87/97/SZ 07 Purbeck, 1970

7   The butt of a firing range catches
    projectiles which have passed the
    target.

8   Martin Papworth, personal
    communication

9   See for example: Ashbee, P. and
    Dimbleby, G.W., 1959 and below p
    129

10 Sunter and Woodward, 1986

11 Interim information on the Internet
    at http://www.bestwall.co.uk

12 Cunliffe, 1987

13 Beavis, 1970; Williams 2002

14 Sunter, 1986

15 'Oboe' was radio navigation aid

16 Royal Commission on Historical
    Monuments, 1970, 297

17 Cooksey, 1974; Lewer and Smale,
    1994, 60-62

18 A recent introduction to the
    prehistory of Dorset is Gale, 2003

19 A complete wedge pit is visible at
    the foot of the quarry face at the
    extreme western end of Seacombe

20 For a useful introduction to the
    archaeology of quarrying in Purbeck
    and Portland, see Stanier, 2000, 83-109

21 This is mostly caused by the absorption of saltwater spray by the bricks. As the water evaporates, salt crystallises in the surface pores. The force exerted by the growth of salt crystals disrupts the cementing matrixof the brick

22 p 110

23 The best general introduction to the medieval and post-medieval landscape archaeology of Dorset is still Taylor, 1970

24 Hinton and Trapp, 2002

25 In the possession of Dr W.H. Penley

26 Oral testimony by Dr W.H. Penley, deposited in the collection of the Oral History Research Unit, Bournemouth University

27 Beavis, Cox and Woodward, 1983

28 Graham, Hinton and Peacock, 2002

29 Royal Commission on Historical Monuments, 1970, 630

30 See for example: Batt, 1991; Lovell, 1991. The Oral History Research Unit at Bournemouth University holds a collection of personal testimony, written and oral, on this topic, some of which is illustrated on its website: http://ohru.bournemouth.ac.uk. Latham and Stobbs 1996 and 1999 also draw on this material

31 See Figure 23

32 See Graham, Hinton and Peacock, 2002, for an indication of the kind of evidence that might be expected if the site were excavated

33 Royal Commission on Historical Monuments, 1970, 630

34 Cunliffe and Phillipson, 1968

35 Woodward, 1986

36 p 59

37 Simms, 1999, 1-6; Stanier, 2002, 35-37

38 Simms, 1999, 31

39 Simms, 1999

40 Crossley, 1987

41 These techniques enable the mineral composition of the ceramic to be determined. The first involves making a thin section of the intact material. In the second the material is ground then 'heavy' minerals are separated from 'light' minerals by floatation in a liquid of high specific gravity. In both cases the minerals are identified using a polarising microscope, and their relative proportions can, in many cases, be matched with those of the source materials from which they have come. See Herz and Garrison, 1998, 248-270

42 'Section', in the sense that an archaeological excavator would use the term: a vertical cutting displaying the relationship between layered deposits and associated features

43 The minerals in fresh shale contain iron in the Fe^{2+} oxidation state and are mostly greyish. On heating in oxygen, these are oxidised to reddish minerals in which iron is in the Fe^{3+} state

44 For fuller treatment see Wills, 1985, or Brown et al., 1995, 79-84

45 In an unpublished survey, 1984, Peter Cox, personal communication

46 Taylor, 1970, 60-62

47 For summary, see Royal Commission on Historical

Monuments, 1970, 612

48 *Mortaria* are vessels, used with a pestle, similar in appearance and function to the utensil used today for macerating resistant culinary or medicinal ingredients

49 Sunter, 1986

50 Royal Commission on Historical Monuments, 1970, 489

51 The technical term for this is 'cross-ridge dyke'.

52 Calkin, 1948, 44

53 Royal Commission on Historical Monuments, 1970, 491

54 Causewayed Enclosures seem to have acted as central gathering places for dispersed farming groups; the nearest lie beneath the Iron Age Hillforts of Maiden Castle and Hambledon Hill.

55 Royal Commission on Historical Monuments, 1970, 489-492

56 Military symbols identifying protected ancient monuments

57 Wheeler, 1953

58 Grinsell, 1959, 165

59 RCHM, 1970, 628-629; Tracy, 1987

60 Tracy, 1987, 22

61 I am indebted to Prof. Vincent May for debating this with me in the field.

62 Soane, 1987

63 Cooksey, 1974

64 p. 77

65 Royal Commission on Historical Monuments, 1970, 183

66 Rahtz, 1959

67 Brown et al., 1995, 36

68 National Trust plan courtesy of Martin Papworth, and Brown et al., 1995, 41

69 1969 Edition, Ordnance Survey, 1:25,000 Series, Sheet SY68/78

70 pp 34ff; 41

71 Lanning, 1989; Pomeroy, 1995, 107

72 Crocroft and Thomas, 2003, 84ff

73 See Crocroft and Thomas, 2003, 139-142, for a general outline of the technique.

74 Pomeroy, 1995, 83

75 Whitley, 1943

76 Royal Commission on Historical Monuments, 1970, 616

77 Royal Commission on Historical Monuments, 1970, 337-339

78 For a detailed description of Portland and Weymouth railways, see Jackson, 1999 and 2000

79 Jackson, 2000, drawing on p.110

80 Latham and Stobbs, 1996, 223

81 Cocroft and Thomas, 2003, 84ff

82 Jackson, 1999, 122 and 65

83 Royal Commission on Historical Monuments, 1970, 252

84 Defence of Britain Database, ID S0005836

85 Stanier, 2000, 104-105

86 Palmer, 1977, 145-148

87 Palmer, 1970

88 Ordnance Survey Outdoor Leisure map Sheet 15, Purbeck and South Dorset, 1999

89 Cocroft and Thomas, 2003, 180-186

90 Pomeroy identifies this as a searchlight emplacement (1995, 91), Legg 2002, 70 with rocketry.

91 Latham and Stobbs, 1996, 223

92 Palmer, 1964 and 1967

93 Bailey, 1963

94 Thomas, 1995, 63

95 Cocroft and Thomas, 2003, 181

96 Beavis, 1974

97 Royal Commission on Historical Monuments, 1952, 10

98 Radcliff, 1996, 59

99 Greenfield, 1985

100 Bailey, 1986

101 Stanier, 1994 and 1996

102 Grinsell, 1959, 97

103 Defence of Britain database, ID S0009070

104 Gelling, 1977

105 Gale, 2003, 122-124

106 CBA Wessex News, September 2003, 18

107 For a description of the technique see Dumane-Peaty, 2001

108 For a description of the technique see Taylor, 2001

109 Papworth, 1994

110 Stanier, 1994, 48

111 Torrington, 1991. This probably unpublished account is a personal recollection of the Battery and, includes a sketch plan identifying the function of many of the buildings.

TWO: CHRONOLOGICAL OUTLINE

1 'Mesolithic' along with 'Neolithic', 'Bronze Age' and 'Iron Age', are archaic terms which originated in the infancy of prehistory when chronology was based on the evolution of material culture. Arguably, they are obsolescent, but they are still useful shorthand for imprecise partitioning of the remote past.

APPENDIX

1 Think of the mobile phone, text message, and the recently acquired virtuosity of young thumbs.

BIBLIOGRAPHY

Ashbee, P. and Dimbleby, G.W., 1959. 'The Excavation of Round Barrow on Chick's Hill, East Stoke Parish, Dorset'. *Proceedings of the Dorset Natural History and Archaeological Society*, 80, 146-159.

Bailey, C.J., 1963. 'An Early Iron Age 'B' Hearth Site Indicating Salt Working on the North Shore of the Fleet at Wyke Regis'. *Proceedings of the Dorset Natural History and Archaeological Society*, 84, 132-136.

Bailey, C.J., 1986. 'The Romano-British Site at Walls, Puncknowle, Dorset'. *Proceedings of the Dorset Natural History and Archaeological Society*, 107, 55-86

Batt, R., 1991. *The Radar Army: Winning the War of the Airwaves*. London: Robert Hale.

Beavis, J., 1970. 'Some Aspects of the Use of Purbeck marble in Roman Britain'. *Proceedings of the Dorset Natural History and Archaeological Society,* 91, 181-204.

Beavis, J., 1974. 'Excavations at the Abbotsbury Castle Hillfort'. *Proceedings of the Dorset Natural History and Archaeological Society*, 96, 56.

Beavis, J., Cox, P., and Woodward, P. 1983. 'An Iron Age Storage Pit Near St Aldhelm's Head, Worth Matravers'. *Proceedings of the Dorset Natural History and Archaeological Society*, 104, 179.

Brown, I., Burrage, D., Clarke, D., Guy, J., Hellis, J., Lowry, B., Ruckley, N., Thomas, R., 1995. *20th Century Defences in Britain: an introductory guide*. York: Council for British Archaeology.

Calkin, J.B., 1948. 'The Isle of Purbeck in the Iron Age'. *Proceedings of the Dorset Natural History and Archaeological Society*, 70, 29-59.

Cocroft, W.D. and Thomas, R.J.C., 2003. *Cold War: Building for Nuclear Confrontation 1946-1949*. Swindon: English Heritage.

Cooksey, A.J.A., 1974. *The Development of Communications in the Dorset Area, Pt V: Admiralty Coastal Signal Stations and Telegraphs in Dorset*, Booklet 607. Dorchester: Dorset Education Committee.

Crossley, D., 1987. 'Sir William Clavell's Glass House, at Kimmeridge, Dorset: the Excavations of 1980-81'. *Archaeological Journal*, 144, 340-382.

Cunliffe, B. and Phillipson, D.W., 1968. 'Excavations at Eldon's Seat, Encombe, Dorset.'

Proceedings of the Prehistoric Society, XXXIV, 191-237.

Cunliffe, B., 1987. *Hengistbury Head, Dorset. Vol. 1, The Prehistoric and Roman Settlement 3500 BC-AD 500*. Oxford: Oxford University Committee for Archaeology, Monograph No 13.

Defence of Britain database: http://ads.ahds.ac.uk/catalogue/specColl/dob

Dumane-Peaty, L., 2001. 'Human Impact on Vegetation', in Brothwell, D. and Pollard, A.M. (Eds.). *Handbook of Archaeological Sciences*. Chichester: Wiley, 379-392.

Gale, J., 2003. *Prehistoric Dorset*. Stroud: Tempus.

Gelling, P., 1977. 'Excavations on Pilsdon Pen, Dorset, 1964-71'. *Proceedings of the Prehistoric Society*, 43, 263-286.

Graham, A.H., Hinton, D.A., and Peacock, D.P.S., 2002. 'The excavation of an Iron Age and Romano-British settlement in Quarry Field, south of Compact Farm, Worth Matravers, Dorset', in Hinton, D.A., (Ed.), *Purbeck Papers*. Oxford: Oxbow Books.

Greenfield, E., 1985. 'The Excavation of Three Barrows at Puncknowle, Dorset, 1959'. *Proceedings of the Dorset Natural History and Archaeological Society*, 106, 62-76.

Grinsell, L.V., 1959. *Dorset Barrows*. Dorchester: Longmans.

Hertz, N., and Garrison, E.G., 1998. *Geological methods for Archaeology*. Oxford: Oxford University Press.

Hinton, D.A. and Trapp, H., 2002. 'The Worth Matravers Strip Fields in the Eighteenth Century', in Hinton, D.A., (Ed.), *Purbeck Papers*. Oxford: Oxbow Books.

Jackson, B.L., 1999. *Isle of Portland Railways, Volume one: The Admiralty and Quarry Railways*. Usk: Oakwood Press.

Jackson, B.L., 2000. *Isle of Portland Railways, Volume two: The Weymouth and Portland Railway; The Easton and Church Hope Railway*. Usk: Oakwood Press.

Lanning, G, 1989. 'The RAF Station at Ringstead'. *Somerset and Dorset Notes and Queries*, XXXII, Part 330, 795-796.

Latham, C. and Stobbs, A., 1996. *Radar: A Wartime Miracle*. Stroud: Sutton Publishing.

Latham, C. and Stobbs, A., 1999. *Pioneers of Radar*. Stroud: Sutton Publishing.

Legg, R., 2002. *The Jurassic Coast*. Wincanton: Dorset Publishing Company.

Lewer, D., and Smale, D., 1994. *Swanage Past*. Chichester: Phillimore.

Lovell, B., 1991, *Echoes of War: the story of H_2S radar*. Bristol: Adam Hilger

Palmer, S.L., 1964. 'Prehistoric Stone Industries of the Fleet-Area, Weymouth'. *Proceedings of the Dorset Natural History and Archaeological Society*, 85, 107-115.

Palmer, S.L., 1967. 'Trial Excavations in the Fleet-Area, Weymouth'. *Proceedings of the Dorset Natural History and Archaeological Society*, 88, 152-157.

Palmer, S.L., 1970. 'The stone age industries of the Isle of Portland, and the utilisation of Portland Chert as an artefact material in southern England'. *Proceedings of the Prehistoric Society*, XXXVI, 82-115.

Palmer, S.L., 1977. *Mesolithic cultures of the British Isles*. Poole: Dolphin Press.

Papworth, M., 1994. 'Excavations of a Bronze Age Round Barrow and Napoleonic Signal Station at Golden Cap, Stanton St Gabriel'. Proceedings of the Dorset History and Archaeological Society, 115, 51-62.

Pomeroy, C., 1995. *Military Dorset Today*. Peterborough: Silver Link Publishing.

Radcliffe, F.M., 1996. 'Archaeology and Historical Landscape in West Dorset from the Air'. *Proceedings of the Dorset Natural History and Archaeological Society*, 117, 51-66.

Rahtz, P.A., 1959. 'Holworth Medieval Village Excavation 1958'. *Proceedings of the Dorset Natural History and Archaeological Society*, 81, 127-147.

Royal Commission on Historical Monuments, 1952. *An Inventory of Historical Monuments in the County of Dorset*, Vol. 1: West Dorset. London: HMSO.

Royal Commission on Historical Monuments, 1970. *An Inventory of Historical Monuments in the County of Dorset*, Vol. 2: South-East. London: HMSO.

Simms, W.F., 1999. *Railways of Kimmeridge*. Simms: Rustington.

Soane, J., 1987. 'Early Medieval Consolidation: 1066-1149', in Keen, L. and Carrick, A. (Eds.). *Historic Landscape of the Weld Estate, Dorset*. East Lulworth: Lulworth Heritage Ltd.

Stanier, P., 1994. 'Dorset Limekilns'. *Proceedings of the Dorset Natural History and Archaeological Society*, 115, 33-49.

Stanier, P., 1996. 'More Dorset Limekilns'. *Proceedings of the Dorset Natural History and Archaeological Society*, 117, 91-94.

Stanier, P., 2000. *Stone Quarry Landscapes*. Stroud: Tempus.

Stanier, P., 2002. *Dorset in the Age of Steam*. Tiverton: Dorset Books.

Sunter, N., 1986. 'Excavations at Norden, Corfe Castle, Dorset, 1968-1969', in Sunter and Woodward, 1986.

Sunter, N., and Woodward, P.J., 1986. 'Romano-British Industries in Purbeck'. *Dorset Natural History and Archaeological Society Monograph, No. 6*. Dorchester: Dorset Natural History and Archaeological Society.

Taylor, C., 1970. *Dorset*. London: Hodder and Stoughton.

Taylor, R.E., 2001. 'Radiocarbon Dating', in Brothwell, D. and Pollard, A.M. (Eds.). *Handbook of Archaeological Sciences*. Chichester: Wiley, 23-34.

Thomas, J., 1995. 'Building Stones of Dorset: Part 3. Inferior Oolite, Forest Marble, Cornbrash and Corallian Limestones'. *Proceedings of the Dorset Natural History and Archaeological Society*, 116, 61-70.

Torrington, Gunner A.C., 1991. *Notes and Facts on 376 Coastal Defence Battery, Royal Artillery, Timber Hill, Lyme Regis, 1940*. Unpublished (?) manuscript, National Trust collection, Warminster.

Tracy, C., 1987. 'Prehistoric Land-Use and Settlement' and 'Dating Considerations and the Relationship of the Barrows to the Celtic Fields', in Keen, L. and Carrick, A. (Eds.). *Historic Landscape of the Weld Estate, Dorset*. East Lulworth: Lulworth Heritage Ltd.

Wheeler, R.E.M., 1953. 'An early Iron Age "Beach-Head" at Lulworth, Dorset'. *Antiquaries Journal*, XXXIII, 1-13.

Whitley, M., 1943. 'Excavations at Chalbury Camp, Dorset, 1939'. *Antiquaries Journal*, XXII, 98-121.

Williams, D.F., 2002. 'Purbeck marble in Roman and Medieval Britain', in Hinton, D.A., (Ed.), *Purbeck Papers*. Oxford: Oxbow Books.

Wills, H., 1985. *Pillboxes: a Study of UK Defences 1940*. Barnsley: Leo Cooper.

Woodward, P.J., 1986. 'Excavations of an Iron Age and Romano-British Settlement at Rope Lake Hole, Corfe Castle Dorset', in Sunter and Woodward, 1986.

INDEX

Abbotsbury 79, 101, 107, 112-115, 140-142
Abbotsbury Castle 16, 112, 117-118, 137-138, 152
aircraft 34, 41, 78, 88, 101, 142
Alan-Williams turret 28
ammunition 14, 91
animal bones 47-48, 136
anti-aircraft gun batteries 142
anti-invasion defences 12-13, 52, 69, 112
antiquarians 68, 118
anti-tank blocks 53, 63, 112, 142
anti-tank defences 13

Ballard Point 15-16
bank 12, 16, 19, 34, 58, 62, 65, 67-69, 79-80, 91, 117, 121, 126, 135-138
barrows 18, 27, 38, 68, 71-72, 77, 80, 82, 117-118, 123, 125, 129-131, 146, 152-155
  long barrows 27, 77, 82, 135-137
  round barrows 27, 38, 72, 82, 117-118, 137, 146, 152, 154
Bindon Hill 35, 67-68, 70-73, 137-138, 142
bituminous shale 54, 141
Black burnished ware 20, 139
Black Head 80
Blacknor Fort 101, 141
blacksmith's forge 32
blast proofing 34
boats 27, 29, 87
boundaries 13, 43, 61-63, 82, 86, 126, 138, 144
  field boundaries 39, 60, 64, 72, 83, 123, 126-127, 130
  land boundaries 61-63, 138
bracelets 45, 47, 121
brickwork 33, 57
bridge 86, 103
briquetage 48, 59, 109

bronze 16, 121, 137
Bronze Age 17-18, 27, 38, 43-45, 72, 113, 126, 129, 137-138, 151
Bronze Age barrows 27, 68, 71, 80, 117-118, 125, 129, 146, 154
bunker 75, 77-78, 91, 101
burial mound 17, 27, 38, 44, 124, 137
burials 38, 126, 129, 135-137
buried sediments 134

Cain's Folly 131, 142
camouflage 14, 77, 92, 110, 113, 117, 133, 142
castles 97
  Abbotsbury Castle 79, 101, 107, 112-115, 140-142
  Corfe Castle 20, 21, 54, 64, 92, 96, 154, 155
  Lulworth Castle 64
  Maiden Castle 135, 150
  Portland Castle 88, 141
  Rufus Castle 96, 140-141
  Sandsfoot Castle 85, 88, 140-141
  Strangways Castle 113
Causewayed Enclosures 68, 82, 135-136, 138, 150
celtic fields 37, 43, 45, 62, 72, 126, 138, 155
Chain Home 34, 77-78,
Chain Home Low 34, 107
chalk downland 19, 82
chert 99, 109, 130, 154
Chesil Beach 88, 112-113, 122
church 62, 110, 90, 140
Clavel Tower 45, 50, 56
cliff quarries 27, 50, 97, 99
climate 18, 20, 76, 134
coal 29, 47, 54, 121
coastal defence forts 85, 96, 141
coastal defence radar 92, 133
coastal defence guns 14, 21, 123

coastal defence gun batteries 79, 142, 155
coastguards 44, 72-73, 75, 100, 113, 118, 122
coins 121
Cold War 78, 91, 101, 115, 117, 142, 152
common grazing 34, 62
Compact Farm 38, 48, 153
context 12, 21, 49, 59, 62-63, 88, 104, 126, 143, 146, 148
crane 29. 92, 99
cremation 137
cropmark 40-41
cross-ridge dyke 16, 69-70, 73, 150

Dancing Ledge 27
dating 17, 76, 129-130, 154, 155
D-Day, preparation for 14, 86, 88, 142
deforestation 18-19, 129
derrick 92, 97
deserted medieval village 110, 140
ditch 16, 17, 19, 23, 58, 62, 64-65, 67-72, 75, 80, 83, 88, 117, 126, 135, 138
downland 18-20, 82, 140
Dragon's Teeth *see* anti-tank defences
dry stone wall 23-24, 38, 43, 84, 118-119, 123
dugout 83
Durlston Head 21-22
Durotrigians 67, 126, 139

earthworks 15-16, 35, 37, 39, 63-64, 67-70, 72, 75, 79, 91, 130, 138
East Fleet 110, 140
East Weares Battery 141
Eldon's Seat 44, 46-47, 153
Emmett's Hill 37-38, 40-41, 43, 137, 139
Encombe Estate 46
erosion 22, 38, 45, 48, 52, 55-56, 63, 82, 126, 129, 131, 133
Europe 9, 20, 24, 78, 134, 144
excavation 7-8, 20-21. 27. 38. 45. 47-48, 54, 62-63, 65, 72, 76, 82, 99, 109, 117-118, 126, 129-130, 138, 152-155

farm 22, 40-41, 43-45, 47-48, 62-63, 112, 127, 130
farmers 19, 33, 43-44, 129
farming 18, 27, 33, 38, 40-41, 61-62, 72, 76-77, 99, 115, 121, 126, 134-135
    arable farming 33, 126, 140
    pastoral farming 140
Ferrybridge 85-86, 88, 92, 107, 109-110
field systems 15, 43, 52, 115, 138, 140

fireplace 32, 104
firing range 16, 50, 61, 110, 142, 148
fishermen 55, 64
flint 47-48, 73, 99, 126, 129, 137
Flowers Barrow 63-65, 67, 118, 142
Fort Henry 13-14, 16, 142
freshwater 21

Gad Cliff 34, 54, 58, 60, 63
Gee stations 41
gemstone 121
glass 53-54, 152
Golden Cap 16, 26, 124, 126-127, 130, 140-141, 154
gorse 17-18
grave goods 38, 118
gun embrasures 11
gun emplacements 14, 16-17, 21, 102, 125
gun ports 96

Hambury Tout 16, 71-72, 118, 137
hamlets 61, 139, 140
heathland 12-13, 17-19
heathland archaeology 12
hedges 62, 80, 84, 123, 126-127, 140
henge monuments 82, 118, 136-138
Hengistbury Head 9, 20, 153
Henry VIII 85
High Angle Battery 91, 141
hillforts 63-68, 80, 82, 112, 117-118, 126, 135, 138-139, 150, 152, 159
hollow ways 75, 110, 112, 115, 124
Home Guard 83, 97
Hounstout 33, 35, 38-41, 45, 139, 142
hunting and gathering 99, 134

Ice Ages 18, 99, 134
industrial archaeology 27, 46
industry 9, 20
invasion 11-13, 24, 88, 107, 126, 130, 141-142
iron 16-17, 46-47, 55, 57, 83, 86, 109-110, 115, 121, 141, 146, 149
Iron Age 9, 13, 15-16, 20, 36-38, 41, 43, 45, 47-48, 55, 59, 63-65, 67-70, 72-73, 80, 82, 84, 109, 112-113, 117-118, 126, 135, 138-139, 150-153, 155
iron stone 141

Jordan Hill 84, 139
Jurassic limestone 38

kilns 20, 121
Kimmeridge clay 35, 41, 44-47, 109
Kimmeridge shale 20, 45, 47, 49, 53, 109, 121, 139
Kingston Down 15, 38, 43, 62, 110, 138

limekilns 121-122, 125, 130, 141, 154
Lulworth Cove 68, 72
Lyme Regis 7, 127, 130-131, 155

masts (remains of) 77, 91-92, 100
medieval farming 77, 115
medieval strip fields 14
memorials 68, 130
Mesolithic (period) 99-100, 109, 126, 134, 151, 154
military training 61, 142
mines 23, 50, 53, 56
mining 23, 49
monuments 9, 15, 17, 27, 82, 112, 129, 136, 148-154
mounds 19, 22-23, 2744, 55, 58, 60, 71, 77, 92, 110, 123-125, 129, 130, 135
Mulberry Harbour (compartment of) 88

National Trust 10, 19, 126-127, 131, 150, 155
Neolithic (period) 18, 19, 27, 68, 77, 80, 126, 135-137, 151
Neolithic farming 135
Nine Barrow Down 27
Nothe Fort 85

Oboe 22, 148
observation post 14, 64, 73, 79, 91, 102, 117, 142
occupation site 37-38, 67
Old Harry Rocks 10, 15
open cast quarrying 23
open-field agriculture 22
Ordnance Survey triangulation station 16
oxen 33, 50
parapet 67, 96
pasture 33, 62, 75, 112, 115, 129
patterns of enclosure 140
Peveril Point 21, 63
Pier Bottom valley 37
piers 53, 56, 86, 103
pillbox 10-12, 15, 28, 50, 52, 57-58, 64, 73, 77, 82, 92, 107, 109, 110, 112-113, 122, 123, 125, 142, 155
pits 16, 19, 23, 28, 38, 43, 65, 67, 75, 83, 92, 112, 115, 118, 124, 138, 148, 152

platforms 21, 44, 69, 75, 86, 101, 117, 130
plough 19, 33, 43, 50, 82, 115
ploughing 15, 33, 37-38, 40, 43, 50, 62, 80, 83, 117, 126, 138, 140
podsols 17, 18
pollen 18, 126, 129, 134
Poole Harbour 9, 12, 20, 139
Portland 38, 41, 44, 60, 79, 85-86, 88, 91-92, 96, 99-100, 104, 109, 134, 140-142, 148, 150, 153-154
Portland beds 27, 35, 54, 58
Portland Bill 16, 35, 92, 100, 127
pottery 47-48, 59, 63, 71-72, 109, 118, 121, 129, 136, 139
pottery making 9, 20
Powder House 44
prehistoric (period) 8, 15-16, 19, 37, 44-45, 47, 72, 82, 104, 110, 126-127, 139, 153-155
Purbeck Beds 21-22, 63
Purbeck limestone 20, 27, 63
Purbeck marble 21, 63-64, 139, 152, 155

quarr cart 23
quarry 20, 23-24, 29, 32, 34, 36, 38-40, 43, 65, 92, 102, 104, 107, 115, 117, 121, 124-125, 141, 147, 148, 153, 154
quarry buildings 23-24
quarry workings 23-24
quarrying 21, 23-24, 27, 49, 88, 104, 115, 121, 141, 148
quern stones 121

radar 34-35, 41, 68, 77-79, 91-92, 104, 131, 133, 142, 152-153
radio navigation 41, 148
railway 49-50, 86, 88, 91, 110, 141, 143-144, 150, 153
railway lines 49-50, 86, 92
rampart 64-65, 67-68, 70-71, 82-83, 101, 117-118, 138
receiver 34, 92
rendzina 19
rifle range 16, 92, 142
Ringstead 75-76, 78, 91, 110, 140, 142, 153
rituals 8, 13, 19, 38, 82, 84, 121, 129, 135-137, 139
roads 12, 27, 40, 45-46, 64, 77, 79, 84-6, 88, 92, 115, 117-118, 125, 131, 139, 143
Roman Army 21, 126
Roman Conquest 21, 138

Romano-British period 15, 20-21, 33, 38, 41, 47-48, 55, 63, 138, 140
Romano-Celtic temple 139
Rope Lake Hole 155
rotor radar stations 142
Round Down 17, 27, 75, 130, 136-137, 141
Royal Observer Corps 73, 100, 117, 142
rut-ways 29

salt 20, 53, 55, 59-60, 149, 152
Sandbanks Ferry 9-10
Sea Fencibles 26, 30, 141
Seacombe 23, 27-28, 57, 148
Second World War concrete 16, 34, 86, 104
section (archaeological) 55-56, 88, 101, 149
settlements 9, 20-21, 34, 38-39, 41, 61-63, 72, 76, 78, 80, 83, 110, 115, 124, 127, 129, 130-131, 135, 137-140, 153, 155
  deserted settlements 61, 76, 78, 140
  medieval settlements 62
Shell Bay 10, 20
signalling station 17, 24, 75, 117-118, 130
slit trench 75
social practice 133, 143-144, 146, 148
soil 17-20, 23, 29, 33, 38, 41, 43-44, 50, 69, 76, 80, 82, 84, 100, 110, 115, 121, 126, 134, 137
  subsoil 17, 43, 100
soil movement 80, 84, 126
space 11, 61-62, 91, 99, 104, 117, 143-144
splitting of stone 28
St Aldhelm's chapel 35
St Aldhelm's Head 34, 41, 91, 138, 142, 152
Stanton St Gabriel 130, 140, 154
steps 14, 24, 33-35, 37, 45-46, 73, 77, 91, 96, 104, 107, 112
stone circles 136-138
stone quarrying 104, 141
Stonebarrow Hill 130, 131, 142
storage pit 38, 43, 65, 83, 138, 152
Studland 7, 12, 14, 17, 21-22, 35, 53, 57, 137, 142
symbol 24, 32, 46, 84, 101, 135-137, 139, 150

Telecommunications Research Establishment (TRE) 35, 41
terraces 14, 23, 29, 33-34, 40, 45, 82, 88, 92, 124-125
terracettes 80
Tertiary sands and gravels 12, 15
tiles 21, 54
Timber Hill 133, 142, 155
tombs 80, 135
tools 32, 38, 47-48, 99-100, 138, 143-144
Tout Quarry 104
trackways 43, 43, 61, 110, 115
tramway 50, 56, 99, 102-104, 141
transmitter 34, 41, 77, 92
transport 27, 53, 59, 88, 92, 97, 104, 118, 141
tropospheric scatter communications 142
tunnel 103

underground magazine 14
Upper Palaeolithic 20
Upton Fort 75
vegetation 18, 65, 68, 78, 100, 115, 129
ventilation shaft 101, 117
Verne Citadel 88, 92
Victorian (period) 88, 91, 101, 146
villages 61, 135, 139, 140

wall/walling 10, 14, 21-24, 33-35, 38, 43-45, 54-56, 62, 73, 84, 91-92, 109, 112-113, 118, 123-124, 130, 133, 142
weathering 16, 33, 69
West Bay 122, 124, 141-142
Westhay Farm 130, 140
Weymouth 79-80, 82-84, 86, 150, 153-154
White Nothe 26, 36, 72, 75, 130, 138, 141-142
Winspit 14, 22-23, 27, 29, 32-33, 37, 43, 50, 75, 92, 97, 140-141
woodland 18-19, 75, 77, 99-100, 129
woodland clearance 33, 127, 129, 134-135, 137
Worbarrow Bay 21, 138
Worth Matravers 34, 38, 45, 77, 152-153

If you are interested in purchasing
other books published by Tempus, or in case you have
difficulty finding any Tempus books in your local bookshop,
you can also place orders directly through our website

www.tempus-publishing.com

or from

BOOKPOST
Freepost, PO Box 29,
Douglas, Isle of Man
IM99 1BQ
Tel 01624 836000
email bookshop@enterprise.net